**Date: 9/9/21**

**248.4 MCD**
**McDowell, Josh.**
**Free to thrive: how your**
**hurt, struggles, and deepest**

"COVID-19 pushed hundreds of millions of people to deeper isolation, especially those struggling with addictions and deep hurts from their closest friends and families. *Free to Thrive* takes you through tested and biblical steps not only to healing but to thriving too."

**—Henri Aoun**, strategic projects leader, North Africa/ Middle East, LifeAgape International

"*Free to Thrive* reveals the God-given call behind our greatest pains and struggles. Josh and Ben help us see the beautiful ways God wired us to flourish here and now, and forever."

**—Kirk Cameron**, actor & producer

"Josh McDowell is one of the best apologists I know. This book is something a bit different though. Vulnerable and honest, *Free to Thrive* helps us understand the hunger and thirst for greater freedom, joy, and wholeness that aches in the deeper parts of our soul and then helps us move toward it."

**—Matt Chandler**, lead pastor, The Village Church, president, Acts 29 Church Planting Network

"In *Free to Thrive*, Josh and Ben provide a proven path to healing from hurt, freedom from what holds you back, and how to experience the flourishing life in Christ that we are created for."

**—Dr. Tim Clinton**, president of the American Association of Christian Counselors

"Many are grappling with how to care for those impacted by anxiety, trauma, and addiction. Thankfully, this book provides clear answers straight from the truth of God's word."

**—Dr. Tony Evans**, president, The Urban Alternative, senior pastor, Oak Cliff Bible Fellowship

"In *Free to Thrive*, Josh and Ben will help you understand God's radical love and purpose for you."

—**Miles McPherson**, senior pastor, Rock Church

"Profound, timely, and one of the clearest books on growth, healing, and why truth matters."

—**J. P. Moreland**, distinguished professor of philosophy, Talbot School of Theology, author of *Finding Quiet*

"The pages ahead are a key to unlock a cage that many don't realize they're in. Others have sadly given up all hope of getting out. Through the vulnerability and expertise of two very gifted guides, God will show you a clear path so that you are Free to Thrive."

—**Jonathan Pokluda**, best-selling author, pastor, Harris Creek

"*Free to Thrive* is an incredibly important book for all generations. It is raw and it is real, but it is also incredibly hopeful. Through sharing their life experiences, Josh and Ben demonstrate how God can exchange ashes for beauty and in doing so transform a life and change the world."

—**Rev. Samuel Rodriguez**, lead pastor, New Season Worship Center, president, National Hispanic Christian Leadership Conference (NHCLC), author, *Survive to Thrive: Live a Holy, Healed, Healthy, Happy, Humble, Hungry, and Honoring Life*

"Healthy leaders are one of the world's greatest needs today. *Free to Thrive* provides a clear path to deal with your past, understand your unhealthy habits, and move toward the healthiest future."

—**Andy Stanley**, pastor and author of *Better Decisions, Fewer Regrets*

"I have been impacted by the writings of Josh McDowell for much of my ministry, but *Free to Thrive* may be the best yet. Josh and Ben brought clarity to apologetics in the midst of Generation Z's blurred lines and broken boundaries. I will be recommending it for years to come to pastors, youth pastors, parents, and students."

—**Dr. Jay Strack**, founder of The Strack Center
for Global Leadership & Ministry at
Charleston Southern University, president/
founder of Student Leadership University

"If you're looking for a winsome, compassionate, and insightful perspective on life's pain, healing, and apologetics, this book is perfect for you. It's timely, authoritative, and unique—a terrific resource that's a must-read for the church today. Thanks, Josh and Ben, for this invaluable contribution!"

—**Lee Strobel**, best-selling author, the Strobel
Center for Evangelism and Applied Apologetics,
Colorado Christian University

"It's no secret that our world is facing mental health issues at devastating levels. In *Free to Thrive*, Josh and Ben offer a clear and biblical path to freedom from any struggle that will result in a thriving life of purpose."

—**Rick Warren**, senior pastor, Saddleback Church

# FREE TO THRIVE

## HOW YOUR HURTS, STRUGGLES, AND DEEPEST LONGINGS CAN LEAD TO A FULFILLING LIFE

**JOSH MCDOWELL AND BEN BENNETT**

FOREWORD BY DR. HENRY CLOUD

THOMAS NELSON
*Since 1798*

Published in Nashville, Tennessee, by Thomas Nelson. Thomas Nelson is a registered trademark of HarperCollins Christian Publishing, Inc.

Thomas Nelson titles may be purchased in bulk for educational, business, fundraising, or sales promotional use. For information, please e-mail SpecialMarkets@ThomasNelson.com.

All Scripture quotations, unless otherwise indicated, are taken from The Holy Bible, New International Version®, NIV®. Copyright © 1973, 1978, 1984, 2011 by Biblica, Inc.® Used by permission of Zondervan. All rights reserved worldwide. www.Zondervan.com. The "NIV" and "New International Version" are trademarks registered in the United States Patent and Trademark Office by Biblica, Inc.® • Scripture quotations marked ESV are taken from the ESV® Bible (The Holy Bible, English Standard Version®). Copyright © 2001 by Crossway, a publishing ministry of Good News Publishers. Used by permission. All rights reserved. • Scripture quotations marked KJV are taken from the King James Version. Public domain. • Scripture quotations marked MSG are taken from *THE MESSAGE*. Copyright © 1993, 1994, 1995, 1996, 2000, 2001, 2002 by Eugene H. Peterson. Used by permission of NavPress. All rights reserved. Represented by Tyndale House Publishers, Inc. • Scripture quotations marked NKJV are taken from the New King James Version®. Copyright © 1982 by Thomas Nelson. Used by permission. All rights reserved. • Scripture quotations marked NLT are taken from the Holy Bible, New Living Translation. © 1996, 2004, 2015 by Tyndale House Foundation. Used by permission of Tyndale House Publishers, Inc., Carol Stream, Illinois 60188. All rights reserved. • The Scripture quotations marked NRSV are taken from the New Revised Standard Version Bible. Copyright © 1989, Division of Christian Education of the National Council of the Churches of Christ in the United States of America. Used by permission. All rights reserved. • Scripture quotations marked TLB are taken from The Living Bible. Copyright © 1971. Used by permission of Tyndale House Publishers, Inc., Carol Stream, Illinois 60188. All rights reserved.

Any internet addresses, phone numbers, or company or product information printed in this book are offered as a resource and are not intended in any way to be or to imply an endorsement by Thomas Nelson, nor does Thomas Nelson vouch for the existence, content, or services of these sites, phone numbers, companies, or products beyond the life of this book.

The information in this book has been carefully researched by the authors, and is intended to be a source of information only. While the methods contained herein can and do work, readers are urged to consult with their physicians or mental health professionals. The authors and the publisher assume no responsibility for any damages incurred during or as a result of the use or application of the information contained herein.

The names and identifying characteristics of some individuals have been changed to preserve their privacy.

ISBN 978-0-310-12335-4 (audiobook)
ISBN 978-0-310-12334-7 (eBook)

**Library of Congress Cataloging-in-Publication Data**
ISBN 978-0-310-12333-0

*Printed in the United States of America*

21 22 23 24 25 26 27   LSC   10 9 8 7 6 5 4 3 2 1

*To the hurting, lonely, and struggling. To the
doubting, questioning, and confused. To those
searching for wholeness, your purpose, and greater
flourishing. May you experience healing, wholeness,
and a thriving life—and know and be known by
the One who makes it all possible.*

# CONTENTS

## Authors' Note

The personal experiences in this book are from both authors' lives. In cases where it is important for the reader to know which of us is relating the story, we will identify (Josh) or (Ben). In other cases, however, it will be left to the reader (if necessary) to discern that information from the context.

# FOREWORD
## There Really Is Hope

Hope deferred makes the heart sick,
but a longing fulfilled is a tree of life.
—*Proverbs 13:12*

**A**s I read Josh and Ben's book, I could not think of another verse that better encapsulates its message. The book you are reading is a story of humanity, of how abuse and other horrible realities of this life can leave us stuck with an unmet longing for relief from the pain, frustration at not even knowing where to begin to stop the pain, and an intense yearning for a good life that does not seem to be forthcoming. Many people can attest to those realities . . . to hurting, being unable to stop the hurting, not knowing how to stop it, and losing hope for a good life past the pain.

But there is good news.

Neither the verse I quoted above or this book end with "hope deferred" or a healing that never comes. Instead, the verse ends with a very powerful promise—that a "desire fulfilled is a tree of life." In other words, when we find the answers to end the pain, a source of life grows within us—one that continues to blossom, yielding fruit throughout the future. Healing that comes through meeting your unmet longings becomes a tree of life. And this is the truth that Josh and Ben's stories reveal. Things can be bad, but when our very real God-given desires are met in a life-giving way, healing comes.

When I first met Josh, as he will describe in this book, he was not what you would consider a "mess" of a life. On the contrary, he was incredibly accomplished—an author who had sold millions of books and a speaker who had spoken to more young people than almost anyone alive at the time. In addition, he had pioneered a path for intellectuals to learn that finding faith and having a brain are not incompatible. He had shown there are real reasons why our faith is dependable, historically reliable, and trustworthy, reasons which had provided great help for millions of people. Josh was happily married and a family man, and he was widely loved and respected.

But as he describes in the book, there were some things that were just "off." There were areas of pain and struggle that—despite his intellect and success in life and work—were still very much hindering his life. As he puts it, these areas left him in a constant state of emotional and physical exhaustion. In those arenas, we see that "hope was very much deferred," and his "heart was sick." I remember thinking, "no one is immune . . . when you go through things that wound us, you will feel the effects in some way." Even if you are Josh McDowell.

But there was another truth right in front of me. I knew that *nothing* Josh was describing was not able to be understood or healed. I knew that God had given us the path to healing that Josh needed, and I had total hope and certainty that he would find it. And that is how the two of us began our journey together.

Over time I was able to see how Josh was committed to the process. And alongside him, I witnessed what I've seen with countless individuals: God has a path of healing, and if we can find it and enter into it, it *works*. God works. He heals. And Josh, to his credit, put all he learned into practice. He looked at

Scriptures that he had never thought would apply to his suffering and put them into practice.

Several years ago I also had the joy of spending time with Ben, the other author of this book, and I learned about his own healing journey. I was greatly encouraged to see an individual who had sought healing and freedom in his early twenties succeed at applying the principles he shares in this book and finding freedom to not only live, but to thrive. I believe his journey and wisdom will also bring you hope and many answers.

As you will see in this book, both Josh and Ben discovered in each of their journeys *that healing is a relational process which involves two key relationships: God, and other people.* So many Christians miss that second point. They miss that we have real God-given longings that are designed to be met not only by God, but also by his people. Healing requires relationships with others. We need one another. I am so glad this book communicates that truth over and over.

So if you are feeling "hope deferred" and have a sick and weary heart, know there is real hope available. And as you will find in reading this book, your wounds and needs are real and valid, but there is healing for both! And that gives us hope, real hope for today.

*Henry Cloud, PhD*
*Los Angeles, CA*

# INTRODUCTION

Something wasn't right.

The ministry God had given to me (Josh) as a speaker, author, and Christian apologist was thriving. I had a team of people reaching the world with me. I'd written many books that sold millions of copies, spoken to millions of people worldwide, and seen thousands accept Jesus Christ into their lives. My team and I had conducted national campaigns to reach youth with the truths of Scripture and the life-changing message of Christ. I had a beautiful family and great relationships with my wife and kids. It seemed as if life couldn't get any better. But I knew that something wasn't right.

I felt constantly on the verge of emotional and physical exhaustion. I agreed to speaking and ministry opportunities for which I really had no time or energy. I said "yes" to helping people with their problems at my own expense. I found it nearly impossible to say "no," but had no idea why. I was burning out. Something had to change. I couldn't function this way any longer. I hit my breaking point.

Unsure of what else to do, I called a close friend—and the best psychologist I knew—Dr. Henry Cloud. I asked to meet with him, and he agreed. Over the course of a year, I made the two-hour trek back and forth to his office almost weekly. He assured me that, together, we could find out what was going on in my life. He promised that God could bring me to a better place. He helped me understand the deep unmet longings of my heart that had compounded from childhood and the destructive wake I was leaving behind as a result of attempting to cope with these longings on my own.

You see, I grew up on a farm in rural Michigan. My dad was the town drunk and he would often turn violent, going on a rampage and beating my mom. There were times when I thought he was going to kill her. I began sticking up for her verbally as early as six or seven years of age, and eventually started taking him on physically when I got older. If I hadn't rescued her during those times, she probably would have ended up dead.

My mom was an overbearing woman and the disciplinarian of the family. She was often unengaged emotionally and quick to point out my wrongs. Since my dad wasn't much of a husband to her, she began to turn to me to carry out many responsibilities around the house, including tending to her emotional needs. I felt a sense of worth and love only when I could rescue her from my dad and meet her needs.

When I was six years old, my parents hired a man named Wayne Bailey to do all the housework my mother couldn't do due to her excessive weight. Within weeks of being hired, Wayne started molesting me. He came looking for me at every opportunity. If I was alone in the barn or elsewhere on the farm, he became a hunter in search of his prey. Sometimes I'd wake up early in the morning to him sitting on the edge of my bed, fondling me. Wayne continued sexually abusing me for seven years. I tried telling my mom, but she didn't believe me. The first time I said something to her, she called me a liar. She made me take my shirt off, and for thirty minutes she whipped me until my back hurt so badly that I cried out, "I'm lying! I'm lying!" I buried the abuse deep within me, swearing to never tell anyone again.

Those experiences crushed me. I constantly felt like there was something deeply wrong with me. No one entered my world as a little boy to understand and get to know me. No one affirmed me for who I had been created to be. I seldom received the love and affection a child needs. I don't say this to blame anyone, but these were harsh realities I had to accept.

Through Dr. Cloud's help, I came to grips with the deep and lingering hurt from these experiences. Although I thought I had left them in the past, I had actually buried them alive. But I could never bury the deep unmet longings I felt for appreciation, acceptance, and safety. Instead, I sought to meet these longings in unhealthy ways. I developed unwanted behaviors such as a short temper and a deep desire to please other people at all costs. I was trying to fulfill my unresolved longings from the past through ministry success, but rather than satisfying my longings, those efforts left me feeling exhausted, angry, and full of shame. I thank God for providing a friend and therapist who was able to kickstart my journey to healing and freedom by guiding me to understand my unmet longings and unwanted behaviors and learn how to have these longings quenched in healthy, satisfying ways.

I share this with you here because after sixty years in ministry, I have seen so many people struggling as I did to live out the relational and moral truths of Scripture. So many individuals struggle to overcome behaviors they hate and yet return to over and over again. It's not uncommon for the average Christian I meet around the world—pastor, parent, or teen—to be viewing pornography and yet so desperately trying to stop. I encounter individuals who are caught in cycles of anger and control and don't know how to break free. And escaping the stress of life to a fantasy world through social media, TV streaming platforms, or gaming? That's a whole different story.

All of this has a direct effect, of course, on the diminishing witness and disappearing credibility of Christians in reaching the next generation. Non-Christians who might otherwise be attracted to Jesus see his followers claiming that Jesus can set them free while they themselves display the same behaviors and patterns as the rest of the world. In our contemporary post-truth culture, where truth is thought of as relative to the individual and people do what is right in their own eyes, hurting themselves and others, Christians must experience healing from their hurts and the unmet longings that drive them to frantically search for any substance, behavior, or relationship that seems likely to meet those needs. Only then can our lives and testimonies appeal to others. This is one reason why, in addition to writing this book, my good friend and co-laborer Ben Bennett and I have launched an initiative called the *Resolution Movement*[1] to help teens and young adults understand and overcome their struggles and experience thriving lives of true wholeness.

Five or six years ago (at the time of this writing), I met Ben Bennett, and I was encouraged by the work he was doing in helping individuals heal from the hurts in their life and overcome unhealthy patterns of thought and behavior. As we continued to stay in touch, God led us to work together. I began investing in him and raising him up to reach the next generation. Prior to his life as a speaker and author, Ben faced multiple addictions, trauma, and mental health struggles in his journey toward a whole and wholehearted life. Through many mistakes, missteps, false starts, and restarts, Ben discovered proven tools and biblical principles that have helped him overcome the hurts and struggles that hindered his journey toward wholeness. For the past decade, he has partnered with world-renowned therapists and ministry leaders, helping individuals young and old understand and work through the underlying factors driving the unhealthy patterns in their lives. His youthful passion and personal journey to freedom from unwanted behaviors and porn addiction, paired with my decades of research and ministry experience, provides a unique combination that can speak to every person's need regardless of age, background, or temperament.

Maybe you're reading this and you've been stuck in unhealthy behaviors, thoughts, or relationship patterns. Perhaps you're experiencing unresolved hurts, shame, or struggles with your view of God. The pain and confusion that these struggles bring can be crippling. Ben and I want you to know that there is hope and real answers that can bring lasting freedom. Or, maybe you're reading this because you have a sense that God has more for you and you want to experience a thriving life—one of spiritual, emotional, and relational health and wholeness. You too will find real answers in this book.

It's high time we face the underlying factors driving our unwanted behaviors and struggles and begin a journey to healing through biblical, well-researched, and time-tested principles. You are not made to flounder and flail; you are made for more. You are made to thrive. Jesus offers you healing, health, wholeness, and true satisfaction. Through timeless biblical principles, backed by research, you'll find solutions in this book that God will use to set you free. We invite you into your journey of healing from hurts and overcoming your unwanted behaviors by engaging your unmet longings. Your thriving life awaits.

# LEGITIMATE LONGINGS

**Y**ou've been waiting your whole life.

Not like Albert Einstein, who worked as a patent clerk while awaiting publication, recognition, and a position as a university professor. Not like Jennifer Lawrence, who starred in indie films until she caught her big break and rose to fame through the movies *Winter's Bone* and *X-Men: First Class*. And not like Beyoncé Knowles, who after decades of hard work became the most-nominated woman in Grammy history.

No, this is not like that. This is the moment you've been waiting for your whole life. It is the cure, the ticket, the answer for which you've been longing and hoping. It is the key to thriving—to being free to thrive the rest of your life.

How many New Year's resolutions have you made? How many promises have you declared to yourself that you would change something, quit something, or improve something about yourself once and for all? How often have you buckled down and told yourself, "This time things will be different"? Was it a promise to start eating healthy and get fit? Finally end a bad habit? Get your priorities straight? Whatever it was, how did it go?

Unless you're one of the rare exceptions, your resolve was

1

short-lived. You initially felt good about the progress you were making until the change became too—what? Time-consuming? Difficult? Exhausting? Costly? Or maybe it was none of those things. Maybe it was simply a mostly unconscious return to the comfort of the way things were before, the way you've always been. Maybe you even shrugged and said, "It's just the way I am."

It might be funny if it weren't so frustrating, even debilitating. After all, we sense that there is more to life than what we're living. We long for better, for more, and we know that our unwanted behaviors and unhealthy habits just aren't getting us where we want to go. Even in our best moments, we crave *a whole life* instead of the halting, halfway kind of life we too often find ourselves living.

## A Cocktail of Compulsions

You're not alone. We have all been plagued by unhealthy habits and unwanted behaviors. We return again and again to the same cycles, even as we desperately and urgently want to change—whether it's the way we treat our bodies, our priorities, secret sin, our relationships, or the "recordings" we play over and over in our minds. Whatever form they take, unwanted behaviors are inherent to the human condition. It's a struggle that has plagued humankind since sin entered the world, and we know that the brokenness and incompleteness we feel is not how things should be. The early church leader, the Apostle Paul, confessed his own struggle around two thousand years ago:

> I do not understand my own actions. For I do not do what I want, but I do the very thing I hate. . . . I have the desire to do what is right, but not the ability to carry it out. For I do not do the good I want, but the evil I do not want is what I keep on doing. (Romans 7:15, 18–19 ESV)

I like to call this the great tongue twister of the faith. "For I do not do . . . but I do . . . I do not do . . ." You get the point. You can hear the frustration in those words, can't you? You can feel the weight of the back-and-forth struggle they express. Paul doesn't understand his own actions. He doesn't do what he wants. He keeps returning to what he hates. He has the desire to do what is right, but he finds himself unable to carry this out, continuing to do what he despises. Can you relate?

Paul, a man who wrote most of the New Testament, who gave his life to telling others about Jesus Christ and was tortured, imprisoned, and despised by religious leaders, found himself stuck in unwanted behaviors. We don't know whether he had in mind a specific behavior to which he turned over and over again, but we see from his words that he was frustrated by what he was doing. Ever been there? #Same.

Our society as a whole is struggling with a cocktail of these compulsions. Twenty-seven percent of adults eat to manage stress in their lives.[1] More than 19 million Americans have strong urges to make repeated purchases and spend excessively, even when they can't afford to.[2] Some studies reveal that as many as 38 percent of the population struggles with an addiction to the internet, using it as a way to get a euphoric feeling while avoiding work or other priorities.[3] Three-fourths of Americans report various symptoms of stress within the last month, such as lying awake at night, irritability or anger, fear, or fatigue.[4]

Mental health issues like anxiety and depression, while categorically different than the struggles just mentioned, are rising among young people. One study revealed that 70 percent of teens say anxiety and depression are major problems among their peers.[5] In one university study,[6] 61 percent of college students reported feeling overwhelming anxiety within the previous year. And 35.5 percent said they "felt so depressed that it was difficult to function." If that wasn't heartbreaking enough, *Psychology Today* recently said, "The average high school kid today has the same level of anxiety as the average psychiatric patient in the early 1950s."[7] The pain of our struggles—the things that inhibit our lives—is real, and we are all struggling with some kind of unwanted behavior or behaviors.

Jasmine, a twenty-year-old college student, had a love/hate relationship with hardcore pornography after being introduced to porn by her friend on the bus in middle school. Jasmine loved God with all her heart, served in her campus ministry, and believed it was wrong to look at porn. But, despite her best efforts to stop, she still sought out hardcore porn several times a week. She felt intense shame for watching it but felt powerless to resist the euphoric feeling of pleasure it gave her. Her unwanted behavior patterns felt inescapable. She knew guys looked at porn, but she thought she was a freak—the only girl in the world who struggled in that way.

She tried countless tactics to stop. She repeatedly promised God and herself that she'd never watch it again. She began praying every day for God to deliver her from her behavior. She tried wearing a hair tie on her wrist; when her cravings for porn surfaced, she'd pull back far on the hair tie and release it to smack her skin. She hoped the pain would help to change her behavior.

Nothing worked. In fact, her failed attempts to stop seeking out porn left her feeling worse about herself. She thought if she could just love God more, if she could just try harder, if she could just be "less of a worthless sinner," she could overcome her secret behavior. Jasmine was caught in a cycle of shame, spiraling downward into depression and anger as she returned to porn over and over again despite her best efforts to change. She didn't dare share her struggle with anyone for fear that she'd be outcast, judged, and shamed even more.

I wish Jasmine could have known that she was not alone. That she was not a freak, not an anomaly. That she was not struggling with a "men's issue." That 76 percent of men and women ages 18–24 seek out porn monthly.[8] That Jesus loved her ferociously despite her struggles and called her chosen, precious, and daughter. That he wanted to engage not only her heart, but also the longings that drove her to porn, and bring about true joy and satisfaction.

Mike, a thirty-seven-year-old husband and father of two, was a self-proclaimed control freak. He knew it, and joked about his control issues when they surfaced, saying things like "I'm on control patrol again" and "I don't struggle with control, I embrace control." But despite his attempts to make light of his struggle, he felt deep frustration at his controlling antics. He expected his kids to pick up and put away their toys immediately after playing, placing them in a gray bin in the corner of the living room. He would get angry when this didn't happen. When Mike had a night out with his friends, he'd get irritated if the location changed at the last minute. If his wife exceeded their monthly budget—even by just a few dollars—he'd fume internally over her behavior, telling himself, "She never thinks about what she is doing with my hard-earned money!"

Mike's men's group at church was well aware of his control issues. He gave the group weekly updates about his worst episodes of controlling behavior and asked them to pray for him. He even adapted the "swear jar" in an attempt to stop his behavior, calling it his "control can." He dropped in a $5 bill whenever he tried to control or lashed out at his kids, wife, or friends. He'd been using the control can for a year, but he continued to feel chained by his unwanted behavior, his grasping for control. The only thing that had changed was that he had started to lash out at the control can whenever he had to contribute to it!

We try so many tactics and techniques to stop our unwanted behaviors. Thousands of tips are offered by experts. Books, YouTube videos, blogs, and sermons at church feed us all kinds of strategies to try. This book, however, while practical, isn't about merely changing our behavior. This isn't a book about behavior modification; it's a book about heart transformation—the kind that Jesus wants to bring about in us as we address the deeper "why" of our hurts and struggles. We will offer a different approach in this book, one based on timeless biblical principles and backed by neuroscience and psychological findings. It's an approach that we've already seen God use to set thousands free, including ourselves. It's an approach that, after more than a half-century of our combined years in ministry, research, partnerships with therapists, and journeys with Christ, needs to be communicated to the world. And it's an approach that forms the basis of a new movement called the *Resolution Movement*.[9]

This approach involves addressing the causes of our unwanted behaviors, the longings behind our sin, idolatry, and bad habits. These unmet longings can drive mental health issues like anxiety and depression.

A longing, simply put, is a persistent craving to satisfy a God-given need or desire inherent to all people. Only when we understand the "whys," the longings, behind our actions can we begin to walk into the freedom God has for us.

## God-Given Longings

Throughout Scripture we see that God has created us with longings for our God-given desires to be satisfied. For example, Psalm 145:19 says, "He fulfills the desires of those who fear him," and Psalm 145:16 says to God, "You . . . satisfy the desires of every living thing." We all have longings, every one of us. These longings are not only common to everyone; in fact, they're actually God-given and, thus, good and beautiful.

We agree with therapists Mark and Debbie Laaser, who wrote in their book, *Seven Desires*:

> We believe that God created us with seven basic, universal desires . . . Having and fulfilling these desires validates our very existence. If these basic desires are fulfilled, we will enjoy a deeper and richer relationship with God and with others.[10]

We long to have our God-given desires met. We feel satisfied and at peace being accepted, rather than rejected, by God and those around us. We enjoy knowing that people appreciate the things we do—a "thank you" is seldom met with anger. It feels good when people encourage us and affirm who God has made us to be with our unique gifts and talents, rather than tearing us down. These God-given longings are not weaknesses. They don't mean we're "needy"; they mean we're human. And they guide our actions. Dr. Dan Allender says,

> Desire lies at the heart of who God made us to be, who we are at our core. Desire is both our greatest frailty and the mark of our highest beauty. Our desire completes us as we become One with our Lover, and it separates us from him and brings death as it wars against his will.[11]

Our longing to have desires and needs fulfilled is beautiful. It's at the core of who we are. God uses these longings to draw us to himself, to know him deeply and intimately. But our longings can also drive us away from him.

Proverbs 4:23 tells us, "Above all else, guard your heart, for everything you do flows from it." Everything we do in life flows from our hearts. All of our thoughts and actions are driven by the longings of our hearts, the things our hearts crave. And God blesses and affirms our longings. But we often seek to satisfy these legitimate, God-given longings in ways that bring destruction or pain, rather than pursuing things that truly satisfy us. By understanding our longings, we can begin to understand how to find the true fulfillment we seek.

As Jasmine started to ask herself what longings she was seeking to satisfy with hardcore porn, she realized that she would imagine herself being the woman on the screen, seducing the guy and having his full attention and acceptance in that moment. For a fleeting moment she was the object of his desire. As she explored further, she started to realize that she would go to hardcore porn whenever she would get into an argument or feel cut down by friends and family. These interactions would leave her feeling rejected and longing to feel accepted.

Once Jasmine started to understand the longing behind her porn use, she began seeking to fulfill that longing in healthy ways. She began combating the lies she was believing about herself. Rather than mentally reinforcing the way she felt with statements like, "They're totally right, I'm not smart enough," or "No one really likes me," Jasmine started reminding herself that she is accepted by Christ: "They may think I'm dumb, but God says I'm fearfully and wonderfully made" and "They may not like me, but Jesus says I am a loved child of God." In moments when she became aware that she was struggling to believe those truths, she'd remember specific instances of feeling close to God and being loved by him. She even gained the courage to start reaching out to safe friends for support to process her feelings and longings rather than immediately going to porn like before.

Mike also began to explore the longings behind his control issues. He realized that often when he went on "control patrol," something had happened that made him feel unappreciated. He saw his anger at his kids for not picking up their toys as a longing for them to appreciate his generosity toward them by taking good care of the toys. When his wife would overspend, it felt to him as if she didn't appreciate his financial provision for the family. When plans would change with friends, he felt like the time he had put into making arrangements was similarly unappreciated.

Mike began to see his longing to be appreciated as a source of his compulsion to grasp for control. He shared this longing with his men's group at church, and they began to be more intentional in thanking him for the things he did. When Mike felt unappreciated, he'd take a few breaths and remind himself of who God says he is. He'd tell himself, "God sees me, God provides for me, the work I do in the Lord is not in vain."

Like Jasmine and Mike, it can be a beautiful thing when we get in touch with our longings. We begin to stop the madness of our unwanted behaviors, and we begin to find what we've been searching for all along. We experience satisfaction and the fulfillment of our longings through God and his people. Understanding our problems leads us to God's provision. God has an incredible way of taking the broken pieces of our lives and making something beautiful out of them.

## A Thriving Life

For most of us, our unmet longings run deep. We live in a broken world where things aren't the way they are supposed to be. We experience the loss of friends and family members; we endure divorce, abandonment, abuse, and assault. We experience embarrassment, shame, and rejection.

The hurts from such unmet longings can be devastating, especially if they are regular and consistent. They can lead to deep caverns of cravings in our souls. These unmet longings and hurts can affect our perceptions of the world around us. We can develop a sense of inadequacy or worthlessness, believing there is something wrong with us. We can think that God is distant, a cosmic killjoy, or obsessed with rules like a parent or authority figure we know. We can come to believe that people will reject us if they know what we're struggling with.

Early in life, I (Ben) was riddled with anger, feelings of worthlessness, depression, and anxiety from my unmet longings. My friends made fun of my weight, rooting in me a deep sense of rejection. My father's frequent anger toward me led me not only to feel inadequate but also to fear for my safety. A lack of knowledge of God's love for me and a lack of security in him led me to greatly fear what would happen when I died.

After I developed Obsessive Compulsive Disorder (OCD), I felt that life had become close to unbearable. Every day was a battle to get through. I was consumed with constant fears about my safety—I feared getting into a car accident or somehow losing my ability to speak and move my body. I feared being embarrassed and rejected by others. I began to doubt that God existed and feared that he would reject me when I died. All of these fears led to certain thoughts and behaviors in an attempt to calm the fears and have a sense of control. For example, if I was walking up a set of stairs and fears came to mind, I felt as if the fear would become reality unless I took action. The only temporary solution for the fear was for me to walk back down the stairs, then walk up the stairs again while thinking about something positive. Each day was consumed with rituals like this any time a fear came across my mind.

What began to consume my thoughts the most were my intrusive doubts about God's existence. I thought that every time I had a doubt, I was instantly no longer a Christian and was doomed to hell. For almost a decade, this was only remedied by praying upward of twenty times a day that Jesus would save my soul whenever I had a doubt. I began to wish that I had never been born, because I thought that would have been easier than the torture and fear I experienced on a daily basis. I was caught in a brutal, hopeless, obsessive cycle of fear.

At times, I could barely sleep for days due to the intensity of my anxiety. Other times, I felt deep sorrow for no apparent reason—an intense grief in which hope and happiness no longer existed. My emotional pain was often so drastic that I feared I'd attempt suicide. It took years to understand the unmet longings that were contributing to all these seemingly random issues in my life. But once I did, Jesus brought breakthrough and freedom like never before.

Uncovering our unmet longings and their effects takes time, so be patient with yourself. We'll dive deeper into these issues in later chapters. The key is to start the process of examining and assessing the longings that underlie your unwanted behaviors.

Then you can start asking yourself, "Why am I drawn to these longings more than others?" Ask, "Where have these longings gone unmet in my past?"

Beginning the process of understanding your longings can be a path to great blessing because God wants to fulfill your desires. He wired you with these longings and designed them to be satisfied in healthy ways, ways that lead to deep healing and wholeness. The greatest tragedy is not the destructive behaviors we choose, but that those behaviors stand in the way of deep relational intimacy with God and others.

In order to pursue the fulfillment of our longings in healthy ways, however, we must discover and live in the awareness of who we are as new creations in Christ. We must live out of a position of wholeness, the completeness of who we are as new creations in Christ. We must find the deepest fulfillment of our longings in Christ rather than always looking to others to satisfy our every need. I love how Touré Roberts defines wholeness:

Wholeness is the state of being complete. It means to be *unbroken*, having no cracks or missing parts that unhealthy and unprofitable fillers can occupy. Wholeness is the highest and healthiest version of any person, a version so awesome that to die before experiencing it would be one of life's greatest tragedies."[12]

Sure, we will never experience complete wholeness this side of eternity. We long for Jesus to return and make all things new, to put an end to brokenness and pain once and for all. But we must live our lives knowing that we have every spiritual blessing in Christ (see Ephesians 1:3) and that God has met the deepest longings of our heart by forgiving us, accepting us, and affirming us. When we bow to Christ as Lord, asking him to forgive our rebellion, he declares us to be a new creation. He sees us as justified—no longer guilty of our wrongs. He declares us as righteous, in perfect standing with all of God's perfect laws. He declares us as his own children who are secure in his love and whom he will never abandon. He declares us complete.

Through God's declarations of us we can go from completeness to completeness. That is, we can live in the knowledge that we are complete in our identity in Christ, while also lining up our attitudes and actions more and more with who we already are in him. We can discover and live in our God-given uniqueness, gifts, and talents, walking into greater intimacy with God and others. We are no longer slaves to sin but slaves to righteousness, and we pursue God's thriving design for life in all areas—a whole life.

Stated differently, we can live from a place of wholeness *into* wholeness. We can grow into the whole and complete person God has already declared us to be. We don't become a new person by changing our behavior; we discover the person we already are in Christ and behave accordingly. Many of us have been urged to start doing things in order to activate the process of spiritual growth. Well-meaning Christians challenge new believers to study the Bible, memorize verses, attend church as often as possible, share their faith with others, and replace old sinful habits with patterns of godly living. Sometimes in our good intentions of wanting to see people rooted in their faith, we convey that their spiritual activity will transform their spiritual identity.

I'm all for these spiritual practices, but studious involvement in these does not transform us. Studying the Bible, going to church, and sharing our faith doesn't cause God to declare us loved or valued. He already has declared us loved and valued because that is who we really are in Christ. We don't *do* our way into our identity as God's beloved children; we *are* God's beloved children. When we realize that we are "God's masterpiece" and learn to occupy that reality, we can live accordingly and "do the good things he planned for us long ago," as Ephesians 2:10 (NLT) says.

God designed us to live a thriving life of wholeness spiritually (being made right with God and enjoying a personal, intimate relationship with him), emotionally (seeing ourselves as God sees us and being in tune with our inner world), and relationally (having relationships of being fully known and fully loved and sharing Christ's love with others). When we are living *from* wholeness and *into* wholeness in all these areas, we begin to experience maximum satisfaction in life. We live according to our design as humans and experience what we were created to experience.

Deep down, all of us want to be happy. We want to live satisfying lives, lives of joy and contentment. Those are the very things God wants for us through his ways. It's time to take off the masks. It's time to embrace the one who invites us into healing and freedom. But we must be willing to expose and surrender our sickness to Jesus, the great physician, and invite others in to support us in our journey. We are only as sick as our secrets. Our shame over our secret behaviors breeds and multiplies in the darkness. We must expose that darkness to the light.

Let us remember that it is the kindness of God that leads us to repentance. When Adam and Eve sinned in the garden, God came after them. It was the radical love of the Father that said to them, "Where are you?" It was the redemptive heart of God that drove him to go after his creation. Similarly, God is pursuing us, wooing us, and inviting us in his kindness, not his disappointment, to turn toward him and toward change. He is turning toward us, and he is turning us toward him.

God is saying, "Where are you?" Come out of hiding. He's not ashamed of you; he loves you; he wants you. He will never abandon you. He wants a relationship with you. His view of you trumps everyone else's. Receive his invitation to be met with healing, grace, and forgiveness.

He created you for wholeness. He created you to reach your potential, to live your life on purpose, to know him and make him known. God created you to find true freedom from bondage and experience true fulfillment, to be free to thrive and enjoy a satisfying life.

# Questions for Reflection

1. What are a few unwanted behaviors that are holding you back?
2. What emotions do you feel about these unwanted behaviors?
3. How do you really feel God views you as a result of these behaviors?
4. Do you really believe Jesus blesses the longings behind your unwanted behaviors and wants to satisfy those in healthy ways?

## CHAPTER TWO

# YOUR SEVEN LONGINGS

**Y**ou walk into your local home improvement store and pause inside the automatic doors to get your bearings. Signs hanging from the ceiling identify the contents of floor-to-ceiling rows of shelves that seem to go on for as far as the eye can see.

You've been there many times before, but the sight never ceases to amaze—and even overwhelm—you. You look around for someone to help you. *Why do store personnel always seem to disappear the moment I enter a store?* Finally, you spot someone wearing the right-colored vest. You head toward her, but she turns the other way. You increase your pace; she walks faster. *Does she know I'm here?*

She turns a corner and you lose sight of her for a moment. You're afraid your quest will end in defeat, but then you see her. You catch up to her.

"Can you help me?"

"Yes, of course. What do you need?"

"Well." You're stymied for a moment. "I don't really know."

"What is it you're trying to do?"

"I don't know that, either. Not exactly."

She seems to be trying to gauge whether you're dangerous in

addition to being crazy. "If you don't know what you need, I don't think I can help you find it."

"Of course." You sigh and rub your forehead. "I just—I'm just not satisfied with the way things are. What I'm doing isn't working, but I don't know exactly what I need."

"I see," she says (but obviously she doesn't). "When you figure out what you need, I'll be happy to help."

You'd never do that, of course. Who among us enters a home improvement store without knowing—at least in general terms—what we need? But as strange as that seems, many of us do something similar in the way we conduct our lives.

We know, as we said in the previous chapter, that there are deep caverns of cravings in our souls. We sense that there is something wrong, much that is unsatisfying, in the way we're living our lives. Whether we're desperate or just generally bothered, we know we need . . . something. But what?

## Beyond Maslow

Everyone needs something. But not everyone knows what he or she needs.

Some of us don't even like to think of ourselves as having needs. We recoil from the notion. We're afraid that having needs makes us "needy"—and no one likes to think of himself or herself in those terms.

But God did not create us as robots. He made us organisms, not mechanisms. This need is evident in the very first pages of the Bible: God designed human beings to have needs. He put the first humans on an Earth and in a garden that was designed to meet their needs. From the earliest moments of human existence the needs for air, food, water, companionship, etc., have been present. And the humans and their needs were part of what prompted God to call his creation "good" (see Genesis 1).

When American psychologist Abraham Maslow formulated

a hierarchy of basic human needs, he simply categorized what the Bible's earliest chapters depict. He suggested that all human beings strive constantly to fulfill certain needs and that we do so in a particular, predictable order. Our most basic needs, of course, are physical: food, water, sleep, breath, etc. When those needs are met, Maslow said humans instinctively and unavoidably seek safety and security—in our persons, as well as in employment, health, property, and so on. Next on his "hierarchy" (usually depicted as a pyramid) are the need to be loved and to belong, the need to feel a part of something and to feel important to someone, and the need to experience a sense of purpose and achievement.

Some people are surprised, when their physical needs are met and they experience a measure of comfort, even prosperity, to find that they still feel dissatisfied. I think this is often because they're still experiencing persistent cravings to satisfy a God-given need that they may not even know they have.

These cravings, or longings, are common to all people. When these needs are met, the abundant life Jesus promised becomes a reality. When he said, "I came that they may have life and have it abundantly" (John 10:10 ESV), he was not promising material prosperity, as some television preachers suggest. Rather, I think he was saying that he is the gateway into the "rich and satisfying life" (John 10:10 NLT), in which all of our longings find their ultimate satisfaction. That satisfaction is found in the forgiveness and new birth that a personal relationship with him offers, and in learning to live the way he designed us to live. This is the life of thriving we were created to experience.

## What Everyone Wants

What are those needs that cause us to feel deprived when they're not met, and fulfilled when they are? We call them the "Seven Longings." Each can be defined by a word or phrase starting with the first letter of the English alphabet. As you read through these Seven Longings, be attentive to the times in your life when these longings were met and when they were not. The greatest fulfillment in life comes when these Seven Longings are met in our lives—and when we get to be a part of meeting these needs for others. Jesus's promise of abundance can be experienced now—not just in the next life—for you and for those you know and love. And the process can start as soon as today.

As we describe the Seven Longings that lead to your unwanted behaviors when they're unmet and to a life of wholeness when they are, our hope is not just to bring about understanding but to lead you to experience the life-transforming power that happens when each longing is met. Since we believe each of these longings is depicted and supported in the Bible, we'll not only illustrate them from our experiences but also lay out the biblical basis for them. We realize that this chapter may seem unrealistically positive, but we want to clearly illustrate that each longing can be met and show what it looks like to have them met.

## Acceptance

Everyone longs to be accepted—to be included, loved, and approved of as you are, no matter what. When this longing is satisfied it makes each of us feel like "I'm valued." We want to know our *being* matters. We cannot truly thrive in life until this God-given longing is satisfied in him and experienced in our relationships with others. Those who have a personal relationship with God through salvation in Christ have experienced his gracious acceptance of us, just as we are, no matter what. Those who come to him in simple faith experience the mind-boggling, life-changing truth of Romans 5:8 (ESV), which says that "God shows his love for us in that while we were still sinners, Christ died for us."

Jesus knew all about the power of acceptance. The Bible describes one occasion when Jesus was swarmed by little children.

His closest disciples, who were in the habit of arguing over their relative importance in God's kingdom, had it all wrong. They apparently thought they had to do something to make themselves acceptable and important to Jesus, and that Jesus would not accept those with no status, no importance, and no influence. So, when people began to bring little children to Jesus to be blessed by him, the disciples tried to put a stop to it. But Jesus said, "Let the little children come to me, and do not hinder them, for the kingdom of God belongs to such as these" (Luke 18:16).

Sally Lloyd-Jones, in *The Jesus Storybook Bible*, writes:

Now, if you had been there, what do you think—would you have had to line up quietly to see Jesus? Do you think Jesus would have asked you how good you'd been before he'd give you a hug? Would you have had to be on your best behavior? And get dressed up? And not speak until spoken to? Or . . . would you have done just what these children did—run straight up to Jesus and let him pick you up in his arms and swing you and kiss you and hug you and then sit you on his lap and listen to your stories and your chats? You see, children loved Jesus, and they knew they didn't need to do anything special for Jesus to love them. All they needed to do was to run into his arms. And so that's just what they did. Well, after all the laughing and games Jesus turned to his helpers and said, "No matter how big you grow, never grow up so much that you lose your child's heart: full of trust in God. Be like these children. They are the most important in my kingdom."[1]

When my (Josh) son Sean was twelve, he played on a Little League baseball team. A week before the season started, I got an idea about how to show him—and his teammates—acceptance. I bought twelve coupons good for ice cream sundaes at a local restaurant and took them to his coach.

"Coach, these are for the kids," I said.

The coach smiled. "This is great. I wish more dads took an interest like this. I'll take them for sundaes after our first win."

"No, Coach. I want you to take them for sundaes after their first *loss*."

The coach looked confused. What I was saying wasn't computing with his concept of winning, losing, and rewards for good play.

"Coach, I don't know about you, but as I raise my kids I don't want to acknowledge their success as much as their effort. And I don't want to acknowledge their effort as much as their being created in the image of God. You see, I believe my son is created in the image of God and that he has infinite value, dignity, and worth, all of which have nothing to do with playing baseball. If he never played an inning of baseball in his life, I would love and accept him just as much."

Sean's coach looked at me for a long moment. Finally, he said, "Well, *that's novel*."

The season started and Sean's team won their first few games. But they lost the third or fourth game, and the coach was true to his word. He gave each player an ice cream sundae coupon and they all went out to "celebrate" together. Sean must have thanked me at least five times for the sundaes, and over the next two weeks several of his teammates came up and thanked me for the special treat. I especially recall a boy named Jessie, who said, "Thanks a lot for the ice cream sundaes, Mr. McDowell. Wow! It doesn't matter to you if we win or not—you love us anyway." Nothing could have made me happier. I wanted to communicate to Sean and his teammates that they were accepted, based not on their baseball skills but upon the fact that they are created in the image of God with infinite value and infinite dignity. Is that kind of lesson too difficult for a twelve-year-old to grasp? Obviously not, especially when you use ice cream to prove your point!

There may be nothing that brings greater joy to the human heart than for another person to know all your faults and failures and accept you anyway, as you are, win or lose, no strings attached. Being approved of, accepted, and included sets us free to be vulnerable about what is broken and painful in our lives and helps us connect and really engage with others.

## Appreciation

Appreciation is the longing to be thanked or encouraged for what you have done. When this longing is satisfied, it helps a person to believe that "I'm capable." We long for acceptance, to know that our *being* matters, and we also crave appreciation—to know that our *doing* matters. Think about the last time you worked hard at something and someone noticed and thanked you—and how satisfying that was. Or maybe it's easier to recall an instance when your efforts were overlooked and unappreciated—and how disappointed and disrespected you felt. Those are the two sides of the appreciation coin, so to speak. Our longing to be appreciated is not just a longing for praise, as important as praise can be; it has to do with *significance*—feeling that what you did or said was important, that your effort and your accomplishments make a difference to someone.

Jesus once took a lengthy and dusty journey, on foot, from Galilee to Jerusalem. As his tired, sandaled feet approached a village, where he might be able to rest or eat, he encountered a group of lepers. Because they were lepers, they had to stay outside the village, in isolation from everyone except other lepers, lest they infect others with their dreadful disease. But when they saw Jesus, the healer everyone was talking about, they lifted themselves onto their feet and began as best they could to wave their hands and shouted as loudly as their failing strength allowed, crying out for his attention to their great and horrible need. And it worked. Jesus stopped. But he didn't even move from the road he traveled. He simply spoke to them, "Go, show yourselves to the priests."

It was a strange thing to say. He said to go into the city, to the temple, and present themselves, according to the Law, so that the priests could certify them as having been truly healed. But they weren't healed . . . until they began to obey. The Bible says, "as they went, they were cleansed" (Luke 17:14).

The story concludes:

> One of them, when he saw he was healed, came back, praising God in a loud voice. He threw himself at Jesus' feet and thanked him—and he was a Samaritan.
>
> Jesus asked, "Were not all ten cleansed? Where are the other nine? Has no one returned to give praise to God except this foreigner?" Then he said to him, "Rise and go; your faith has made you well." (Luke 17:15–19)

Just one of ten said "thank you." And that made an impression on Jesus. He was "in every respect like us" (Hebrews 2:17 NLT), so he felt the slight of the nine who showed no appreciation, and the blessing of the one who did.

Appreciation is a deeply felt human need. It works wonders when we receive it, and when we give it to others. You've seen it when you thanked people on active military duty for their service. Or when you made a special effort to show appreciation for good service in a restaurant. Or when you expressed gratitude to a coworker or employee for a job well done. In fact, a study published in *The Journal of Personality and Social Psychology* by researchers Adam Grant and Francesca Gino described the outcome of four experiments designed to measure the effects of appreciation in the workplace.

> Experiment 1 involved participants editing a student's job application cover letter, receiving either a neutral or grateful email message from the student, and then choosing whether to help that individual on another letter. Experiment 2 examined whether participants would help a different beneficiary after

they were thanked for helping the first student. Experiment 3 looked at how an annual giving director's gratitude toward fundraisers influenced further behaviors in raising money to benefit a university. Experiment 4 returned to the cover letter assistance task, but the gratitude message was delivered or withheld in an in-person interaction. Participants were measured as to how effective they felt they were at the requested task, as well as how valued they felt.[2]

In each of the four experiments, participants reported feeling valued—and more likely to work harder or help more—when they were thanked for their efforts.

While acceptance is the foundation for a secure relationship that leads to flourishing, appreciation can be considered a cornerstone of a "whole" life. What would it be like to work, live, and play with the kind of people who affirmed the big and the small efforts we gave? And to be that person in the lives of others?

You may think, "If I go around expressing appreciation to people for what they do and think all the time, they may think I only like them for what they do or say." This is why acceptance is so important as the starting point for growing and developing vigorously (thriving). We all long to know that our being is enough—this is primary—but appreciation is needed as well.

## Affection

Affection is the longing to be cared for with gentle touch or emotional engagement. It is another universal and acute human need. We all enter this world with a need to be cared for, touched, and engaged with emotionally. When we are, it produces a feeling of "I'm lovable."

A 1944 landmark study conducted in the United States involved forty newborns. The purpose of the study was to see whether the infants could thrive if their basic physiological needs were provided, or if affection was also necessary. They were separated into two groups and housed in different areas. Specific instructions were given for each group's care. In Group I, the caregivers were instructed to feed, bathe, and change the diapers of the infants but to do nothing else; the infants were not to be looked at or touched more than was necessary and the "caregivers" were not to communicate with them at all. All of their physical needs were scrupulously provided, and the environment was sterile; none of the infants became ill. However, the experiment was halted after just four months when half of the infants died.[3]

> At least two more died even after being rescued and brought into a more natural familial environment. There was no physiological cause for the babies' deaths; they were all physically very healthy. Before each baby died, there was a period where they would stop verbalizing and trying to engage with their caregivers, generally stop moving, nor cry or even change expression; death would follow shortly. The babies who had "given up" before being rescued, died in the same manner, even though they had been removed from the experimental conditions.[4]

While this was taking place, in a separate facility, the second group of twenty newborns were provided with basic physiological needs along with caring words, hugs, and kisses from the caregivers. Group II recorded not a single death.[5] The results of the experiment were heartbreaking and tragic, but the conclusion was emphatic—nurture and affection are vital needs in humans.

A few years later, another project by researcher René Spitz influenced a major shift in children's homes and hospitals by filming the effects of emotional deprivation on children. He showed that a child who is deprived of human affection may survive but cannot thrive physically or emotionally. However, when a child is given skin-to-skin contact, care, affection, and proper nurture, the baby's immune system will be strong, his or her appetite will be healthy, and a robust weight gain will result.

No amount of affection is too much for children. Likewise, adults need daily affection and emotional engagement, and the longing to be shown such care never goes away. We see this in the biblical accounts of Jesus and the children, when "people brought little children to Jesus for him to place his hands on them and pray for them" (Matthew 19:13). A gentle touch and words of blessing like this communicate a sense of value and provide emotional reinforcement, helping a person to believe that he or she is lovable. The Gospels repeatedly depict Jesus showing affection by speaking caring and honoring words and giving appropriate physical contact like a hug, a kiss, an embrace—even to his betrayer on the night of his betrayal (e.g., see Matthew 26:49; Luke 12:4; John 15:14–15). And the early church leader, Paul, repeatedly encouraged followers of Jesus to "Greet one another with a holy kiss" (2 Corinthians 13:12; see also Romans 16:16; 1 Corinthians 16:20; 1 Thessalonians 5:26).

Affection is so important to the human soul that God gave us the blessings of both sexual and non-sexual touch. God created us with the longing for appropriate sexual affection and gave us marriage as the safe and sacred place for that form of affection to be experienced. But "I love you" can be said and expressed in a wide variety of non-sexual ways as well—a hug, a peck on the cheek, an arm around the shoulder. Words of affection and appropriate forms of touch connect us with one another and make us feel close.

## Access

Access is the longing to have the consistent emotional and physical presence of key figures. When this longing is satisfied, it gives us the feeling of "I'm important." I will never forget one day when I (Josh) was in my study, busily engaged in several demanding projects at once. I was hammering out a chapter for a new book when my two-year-old son Sean wandered in with a ball in his hand.

"Want to play, Daddy?" he chirped expectantly.

"Son, how about a little later? I'm right in the middle of a chapter."

Sean was too young to know what a "chapter" was, but he got the message: Daddy was busy. Unavailable. He trotted off without complaining and I returned to my manuscript.

Within minutes, my study door soon opened again. My wife, Dottie, came in and sat down.

"Honey, Sean just told me you were too busy to play with him. I know that this book is important, but I'd like to point something out."

"What is that?" My tone wasn't as kind and responsive as it should have been. After all, I was doing "important work."

"I think you have to realize that you are always going to have contracts and you're always going to have deadlines. Your whole life you will be writing and doing other projects, but you're not always going to have a two-year-old son who wants to sit on your lap and ask you questions and show you his new ball."

"Honey, I think I hear what you're saying, and you make a lot of sense, as usual. But right now I've got to get through with this chapter."

"All right, Josh, but please think about it. You know, if we spend time with our kids now, they'll want to spend time with us later."

It wasn't long before I took a break from my writing and found my son. I didn't want to give him the impression that he was less important than a chapter—or even a whole book. I wanted to meet his need for significance by letting him know he had access to me, by being as "present" and available as possible to him.

Having access to someone who is consistently present to engage with emotionally allows us to see and experience that we are important. This has become increasingly challenging in the era of the smart phone. People are alone together. We are hyper-connected, yet lonelier than ever because we crave more than a virtual "connectedness"; we need to know that we have access to those who are important to us, which conveys to us a sense of our worth and significance. The younger we are, the more we need to know that we have access to the important people in our lives, but we never outgrow that need. And, while physical presence is important, being emotionally present is just as crucial.

An incident in the Gospel of Mark may shine a light on this need in our lives, especially at critical times. Jesus and his closest friends and followers had reached the end of a long day of teaching and ministry. They finally escaped the press of the crowd and sailed across the Sea of Galilee in a boat. Jesus lay down in the stern of the boat and soon fell asleep on a cushion. As he slept, however, a furious storm arose, and the waves began to threaten to swamp the boat.

In the midst of the storm, the disciples woke Jesus, saying, "Teacher, don't you care if we drown?"

Jesus rose and spoke to the wind and waves. "Quiet! Be still!"

The wind died, and the sea's surface became calm again.

You may have read or heard that story before, but did you ever notice what Jesus's disciples asked him? They said, "don't you care if we drown?" Sure, they were afraid of the storm and its effects, but the words reveal something deeper: they thought his apparent unavailability meant that he thought they were unimportant. He went on to reveal that such wasn't the case—that it wasn't their significance but their faith that was too small.

Still, in his humanity, even Jesus couldn't be accessible to his followers 24/7, which is why he ascended to heaven after his resurrection and sent the Holy Spirit, saying, "I will ask the Father, and he will give you another advocate to help you and be with you forever—the Spirit of truth. . . . Very truly I tell you, it is for your good that I am going away. Unless I go away, the Advocate will not come to you; but if I go, I will send him to you"

(John 14:16–17; 16:7). In sending the Holy Spirit, Jesus made his presence available to his followers always and forever.

God has implanted in every human soul a longing to know that we are important, and that need is met when we know that someone who is important to us is accessible to us and willing to be present with us. How beautiful it is that God gives us the gift of his Holy Spirit so that we need never feel alone in the boat, so to speak. But he also intends for our need for access to be met through others, which is why the Bible includes more than 150 "one another" statements that encourage God's people to be available to each other (e.g., see Romans 12:10, 16; 2 Corinthians 13:11; Ephesians 4:32). Knowing that people we value are accessible to us teaches us that we are important and significant.

## Attention

Attention is the longing to be known and understood with someone entering your world (by this, we mean someone taking time to recognize and participate in what's important to you such as your opinions, dreams, desires, and interests). When this longing is satisfied, it produces a feeling of "I'm understood." Have you ever entered a full room or a building (or a church) without being noticed and greeted by anyone? Do you remember how that felt? It's a lonely feeling, isn't it?

Every human being longs to be seen, noticed, and understood. We all want someone to enter our world and pay attention to us. Our need for attention isn't a need to be in the spotlight, so to speak; it is a heartfelt need for someone to notice who we are, what we're interested in, what we're going through, and what we're capable of doing and being. And we all long for that and need that every day.

When my son Sean was ten years old, he was intensely interested in sports cars. He would cut out magazine pictures of cars like the Maserati, the Lamborghini, and the Ferrari Testarossa and pin them on his bedroom wall. I wasn't particularly interested in such cars, but I noticed Sean's interest. So one day I decided to surprise him by entering his world. I searched and picked out some of the top sports car dealerships in Beverly Hills, a few hours from where we lived at the time. I sent each car dealer a letter that said:

> I'm a desperate dad. I'll do anything to spend time with my son, and right now he's into sports cars. Would it be possible for me to pull him out of school and bring him up to your showroom so that we could take some test drives? I want to tell you up front, I'm not interested in buying a car. I just want to dream with my son.

Amazingly, I got positive replies from every dealer. I called and made appointments for us, and we drove up to Beverly Hills for a day of riding in insanely expensive sports cars. Sean went on "test drives" and "tried out" just about every sports car imaginable. He was in heaven! Some of the salesmen even gave him posters of the cars he had ridden in, some of which were autographed by famous race car drivers.

On the way home, we discussed which cars we liked the best and went over all the flyers, books, and posters Sean had collected, and I took the opportunity to discuss values with him, in light of the very expensive machines he had ridden in that day. Years later, Sean said to me, "I'm convinced the lesson on what we value in life would have never stuck with me if you hadn't entered my world and demonstrated your love for me by focusing on my interests. The real lesson that day that molded and shaped me as a father and husband is that I am to enter the life of my wife and family in order to love and be loved."

King David wrote, "O LORD, you have examined my heart and know everything about me . . . Every moment you know where I am" (Psalm 139:1, 3 TLB). The Hebrew word that passage uses for "know" (*sakan*) means a caring involvement. God had much more than an informational knowledge of David; he was caringly involved in David's life. God not only knows us and wants us to know him; he wants to be lovingly involved in our lives. In the ultimate display of love, he sent his Son into the world, into *our* world, as a human being, to share our trials, temptations, pains, and pleasures in a way that was beautifully designed to demonstrate his love for us and our importance to him. And he created us to need such attention in our lives, both with him and with those around us.

That longing for attention is why you may feel hurt or insulted when someone calls you by the wrong name—especially if it's someone who should know you. It's why you feel so let down when someone you care for gives you a generic or "re-gifted" birthday or anniversary present. It's why you feel devalued when someone close to you looks around you, talks past you, or stops listening to you. It's also why you feel blessed when someone enters your world, shows an interest in what interests you, and shares your trials, temptations, pains, and pleasures in a way that demonstrates their love for you and your importance to them.

## Affirmation of Feelings

Another need we all share as human beings is the longing to have our feelings affirmed, validated, or confirmed by others. When this longing is met, it conveys a sense of authenticity; it communicates, "I'm embraced." Having our emotions affirmed frees us to feel both the emotional highs and lows of life, which is a big part of thriving. When someone acknowledges what we're feeling, even when that feeling is negative, it has a positive effect, reassuring us that we're not "weird" or "crazy" to feel the way we do.

My friend Ray experienced the transformation that can take place in us when this need is met. His wife, Gail, had been repeatedly bullied by a coworker, and would often come home in tears at the end of a workday. Ray tried to be helpful by telling Gail things like, "You need to tell her to back off" and "You should tell her she's not your boss, and if she continues such behavior, you'll file a formal complaint." All of his suggestions, however, seemed only to fuel the fires of Gail's frustration.

One day, inspired by a friend's wise counsel, Ray decided to respond to Gail's complaints by affirming her feelings. When she arrived home crying, with a new report of fresh outrages committed by her coworker, Ray refrained from giving her any advice. He went to her and wrapped her in a hug, and she laid her head on his shoulder and cried.

"You're angry," he said.

"You're darn right I'm angry."

"You have every right to be angry. You feel disrespected and devalued, too, don't you?"

She lifted her head. "Yes!"

"I would too."

She dried her tears. "You don't think I'm being too sensitive?"

"No. I'd feel the same way."

"I feel like she just wants to hurt me."

"I can see why you feel that way."

A few moments passed, and Gail took a deep breath. "You know what? I need to tell her to back off, and if she doesn't, I'm going to file a formal complaint."

Ray later told me how amazed he felt at the effect his words of affirmation had on his wife. She didn't need his advice, but she was calmed and blessed when he simply affirmed her feelings. He said it felt like "magic." But it wasn't magic; it's simply what happens when this need for affirmation of feelings is met.

A familiar story from the Bible contains an often-overlooked example of Jesus recognizing and meeting this need. It happened one day in the village of Bethany, when Jesus and his closest followers arrived at the home of Martha, Mary, and Lazarus. Martha leaped into action in the kitchen, to take good care of the Rabbi and his followers. But her sister, Mary, placed herself among his followers and sat at his feet to listen and learn as he taught.

Mary's action rubbed Martha the wrong way. It was audacious for her little sister to act like she belonged among the men, as if she could be one of the Rabbi's disciples just like them. But she also left Martha to do all the work of hostess and cook by herself! So Martha went to Jesus to complain.

"Lord, don't you care that my sister has left me to do the work by myself? Tell her to help me!" (Luke 10:40).

Some people see Jesus's reply as a rebuke. But notice that he carefully—and, I think, sensitively—affirmed Martha's feelings: "Martha, Martha," the Lord answered, "you are worried and upset about many things, but few things are needed—or indeed only one. Mary has chosen what is better, and it will not be taken away from her" (Luke 10:41–42).

It would've been nice if the Bible recorded Martha's response, but it doesn't. Did she stalk away in a huff? Did she glare at Jesus? Or at her sister? Or did she feel comforted that, at least, Jesus had affirmed her feelings? He didn't say that her feelings were wrong, though he may have suggested that she was going a bit overboard in her preparations. We don't know the answer to those questions, but I think it's possible that Martha was comforted and reassured by Jesus's words.

Jesus's words, both to Martha and about Mary, embody the truth of Romans 12:15, which says, "Rejoice with those who rejoice; mourn with those who mourn." As the New Living Translation puts it, "Be happy with those who are happy, and weep with those who weep." When someone does this for us, affirming our feelings, we feel embraced and valued, and step further into the thriving life God desires for us.

## Assurance of Safety

In addition to the longings we all feel for acceptance, appreciation, affection, access, attention, and affirmation of our feelings, we also feel a deep need for the assurance of safety—that is, to feel safe, protected, and provided for emotionally, physically, and financially. We crave more than just being told, "Everything is going to be okay." We long for the assurance of our safety and security. We want to feel confident that we will be protected and provided for emotionally, physically, and financially. Mark and Debbie Laaser describe it this way:

> We want to know that we are materially secure—that we have food, and a place to live, and enough money to support ourselves. We want to know that we are spiritually safe—that our God is a God who will not pull the rug out from underneath us, that he is a God who keeps his promises. And we want to know that we are emotionally secure, that those around us are reliable, that those people who say they love us can be counted on to act lovingly.[6]

When this longing is satisfied, it produces a sense of stability in our lives and the freedom to enjoy, explore, and experiment in life without fear. When this need is met, we have a feeling that says, "I'm secure." Both men and women have the need to be protected and provided for emotionally, physically, and financially. If these are not present, it may feel like instability is the air that you breathe.

I think our longing for the assurance of safety is an ache for the Garden, where God provided for every human need (see Genesis 2). However, when our human ancestors fell into sin their fall introduced into their lives every kind of insecurity. It brought fear—"I was afraid." It engendered shame—"Because I was naked." It produced alienation—"So I hid" (Genesis 3:10). Even so, God provided the means for our needs to be met—first and foremost, in him as our Protector (Psalm 46:1) and Provider (Matthew 6:26).

We can find assurance in the simple truth that God exists and that he is our Creator and Sustainer. He has given us a longing for the assurance of safety and security that finds fulfillment in our relationship with him, the ultimate Father and Friend, Deliverer and Defender. As we live in relationship with him, living out the truths of his word that are rooted in his nature and character, we can know that we are provided for and protected by someone who is good and wants the best for us.

God has also designed us to long for and receive the assurance of safety in our human relationships, especially in childhood. In fact, the Bible makes it clear that the early church in Jerusalem was instrumental in meeting this need, as "All the believers were together and had everything in common. They sold property and possessions to give to anyone who had need. Every day they continued to meet together in the temple courts. They broke bread in their homes and ate together with glad and sincere hearts, praising God and enjoying the favor of all the people" (Acts 2:44–47). This passage depicts the early Christians' need for material and emotional security being met through their relationships with other followers of Jesus Christ. It is also a depiction of the way God intends for you to live—a state in which you feel safe, protected, and provided for emotionally, physically, and financially, and free to enjoy, explore, and experiment in life without fear.

## The Wholeness Apologetic

When we experience our Seven Longings being met in healthy ways with God and others, we experience "true wholeness." This forms the basis of what we call the Wholeness Apologetic model pictured on the next page. Throughout this book we will explore each aspect of the model, occasionally referring back to the diagram. We'll explain why we struggle to experience this life of true wholeness we were intended to live and how we can reclaim that divine design.

## THE WHOLENESS APOLOGETIC

Supporting God's design for human flourishing in all areas of life.
We experience this primarily through the fulfillment of our
Seven Longings with God, self, and others.

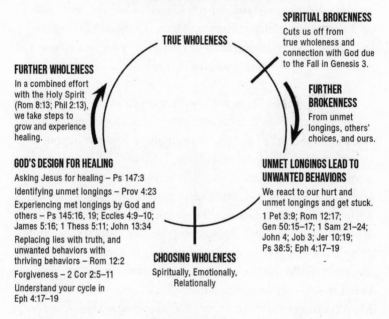

**SPIRITUAL BROKENNESS**

Cuts us off from
true wholeness and
connection with God due
to the Fall in Genesis 3.

**TRUE WHOLENESS**

**FURTHER WHOLENESS**

In a combined effort
with the Holy Spirit
(Rom 8:13; Phil 2:13),
we take steps to
grow and experience
healing.

**FURTHER
BROKENNESS**

From unmet
longings, others'
choices, and ours.

**GOD'S DESIGN FOR HEALING**

Asking Jesus for healing – Ps 147:3
Identifying unmet longings – Prov 4:23
Experiencing met longings by God and
others – Ps 145:16, 19; Eccles 4:9–10;
James 5:16; 1 Thess 5:11; John 13:34
Replacing lies with truth, and
unwanted behaviors with
thriving behaviors – Rom 12:2
Forgiveness – 2 Cor 2:5–11
Understand your cycle in
Eph 4:17–19

**UNMET LONGINGS LEAD TO
UNWANTED BEHAVIORS**

We react to our hurt and
unmet longings and get stuck.

1 Pet 3:9; Rom 12:17;
Gen 50:15–17; 1 Sam 21–24;
John 4; Job 3; Jer 10:19;
Ps 38:5; Eph 4:17–19

**CHOOSING WHOLENESS**

Spiritually, Emotionally,
Relationally

# God's Design

The first crisis in human history occurred after God created Adam
and surrounded him with every possible resource he might need,
except for one: "The Lord God said, 'It is not good for the man
to be alone. I will make a helper suitable for him'" (Genesis 2:18).

Human aloneness was a crisis, an undesirable situation that
God took extreme measures to correct. Adam had all he could
want in that pristine garden, including the presence of God himself. But God is a relational God who made us for relationship, not
only with him but also with other human beings (Genesis 1:26).

One of the world's longest studies ever done was begun in 1938 by
Harvard University.[7] The objective was to discover the key to happiness and health. After eighty years of study, researchers concluded:

"The surprising finding is that our relationships and how happy we are in our relationships has a powerful influence on our health," said Robert Waldinger, director of the study, a psychiatrist at Massachusetts General Hospital and a professor of psychiatry at Harvard Medical School. "Taking care of your body is important, but tending to your relationships is a form of self-care too. That, I think, is the revelation."

In other words, "It is not good for humans to be alone." We all have needs that can be met only through our relationships with God and other people. A flourishing life can happen only in connection with God and others. If all of the Seven Longings are met in healthy ways, you will feel valued, capable, lovable, important, understood, embraced, and secure. You'll experience a life of wholeness. Doesn't this sound like the thriving life we all long to experience? This is possible, but only in the context of a relationship with God and others. Isolated thriving is an oxymoron, like jumbo shrimp or old news. Isolation leads to loneliness, a state in which our longings cannot be fully met. As Dr. Waldinger concluded from the Harvard study, "Loneliness kills. It's as powerful as smoking or alcoholism."[8] And when the Seven Longings we've explored go unmet, our sense of loneliness deepens and results in hurt, hardship, and unhealthy behaviors. What does that look like? This is the focus of the next chapter.

## Questions for Reflection

1. What longings were met in healthy ways before your teenage years?
2. Who were the people who met your longings in healthy ways?
3. What longing are you most thankful was met growing up?
4. If you could have one longing met today, what would it be and why?

CHAPTER
THREE

# YOUR UNMET LONGINGS

On a beautiful spring afternoon years ago, when I (Ben) was fifteen years old, I eagerly anticipated the arrival of the weekend so I could kick back and have fun with friends. I had awakened early for the previous five days in a row, worked hard at school, and completed all of my homework. When Saturday morning finally arrived, I texted my close friend, Cam: "Wanna hang out today?"

Cam answered quickly. "Yeah! Not sure what I'm doing today, but I'll let you know when I figure it out."

A couple of hours passed, and I heard nothing more, so I texted Cam again. No reply. Thirty minutes later, I tried calling. No answer. An hour later, I sent another text. Still no response. I was bored and impatient. The day was quickly passing, and all the hoped-for fun and friendship hadn't materialized.

Finally, I stormed out of the house and hopped on my skateboard to ride over to Cam's house, a mile-and-a-half away. It felt good to be rolling through the neighborhood, but my frustration and curiosity battled each other. Soon, however, I approached Cam's house and could see Cam out front with two of our mutual friends, Taylor and Joe. They were doing tricks on their skateboards and laughing with each other.

"Hey guys. I tried texting and calling you, but you didn't answer."

Cam shrugged. "My phone's been on silent."

*For five hours?* I thought. *While you knew I wanted to hang out, and you all had fun without me?*

Joe spoke up then, a look of disgust on his face. "You can't just come over here, uninvited."

I looked from him to the others, and back again. Cam didn't meet my gaze. Understanding slowly dawned. My heart sank. They wanted to hang out, just not with *me*. They'd been ignoring me. Excluding me. Intentionally. I'd been uninvited. Rejected.

It hurt so badly I can still feel the sting today. What made the situation worse was that it felt like the thousandth time my friends had made me feel like a reject.

I felt sad, embarrassed, and unwanted in that moment. Their previous remarks from the last few years came rushing back to my mind: "Stop being annoying, Ben," "You're so weird," "You're fat," and more.

What happened to me on that memorable day was the deepening of a wound from an unmet need. I longed for acceptance, especially from those I considered to be my closest friends. I wanted to be included, loved, and approved of for who I was, no matter what. So when I felt the sting of rejection instead, it hurt deeply—a hurt that, to a great extent, lingered for many years afterward.

## Everybody Hurts Sometimes

We live in a world where things are not the way they were originally intended to be. We were created for Eden, a paradise without pain, suffering, struggles, or sin. A place where we could know God and others deeply, unafraid of rejection or ridicule—a place of wholeness and thriving physically, spiritually, emotionally, and sexually. But, of course, we don't live in the Eden for which our souls were created.

We live in a fallen world, a broken world, in which our God-given longings often go unmet. We experience loss, grief, pain, and betrayal. People who are supposed to be there for us let us down. Those who are supposed to love us the most often hurt us the most. After all, we are imperfect people interacting with other imperfect people. These sufferings can happen in many different ways, but some of the most consistent and significant ways we experience these unmet longings are in relationships. Sigmund Freud, the "father of psychotherapy," also recognized this reality:

> We are threatened with suffering from three directions: from our own body; which is doomed to decay . . . , from the external world, which may rage against us with overwhelming and merciless force of destruction; and finally from our relations to other [human beings]. . . . This last source is perhaps more painful to us than any other.[1]

In the previous chapter, we explained the Seven Longings and what it looks and feels like when those longings are fulfilled, which formed the basis of the Wholeness Apologetic model. In this chapter, we'll show what it looks and feels like when those longings go unmet (see "Further Brokenness" in the Wholeness Apologetic diagram). As we do, you'll probably find that some descriptions and depictions resonate more with you than others do. This may help you to identify some of the unmet longings in your life—past and present—which eventually may help you come to a greater understanding of the unwanted behaviors in your life.

## David's Dark Chapter

The Bible records many memorable episodes in the life of David, the giant-slayer, court musician, and shepherd-king of Israel.

He was a brilliant and compelling leader, and a passionate lover of God, but he had failings, like we all do, and he had almost constant trouble with his family.

When David was a boy, King Saul's son, Jonathan, was next in line to take the throne of Israel, but God had other plans. God sent the prophet Samuel to choose a king from among the sons of a man named Jesse. When Samuel arrived, he looked over Jesse's sons, but none were who God had appointed to be the next king of Israel. Samuel asked Jesse if he had any more sons; Jesse responded, "Well, yes, there's the runt. But he's out tending the sheep" (1 Samuel 16:11 MSG). The Hebrew word Jesse used to describe his son ("runt," MSG), means young, small, insignificant, unimportant. Apparently, Jesse assumed that David wasn't worth presenting to Samuel! Samuel told Jesse to fetch this son anyway, and when he arrived, the LORD said, "Rise and anoint him; this is the one" (1 Samuel 16:12). David, the seemingly insignificant and unimportant son of Jesse, would be the next king of Israel.

Now, we can only speculate, but it wouldn't be surprising if David had some significant unmet longings stemming from his family situation and his father's attitude toward him. He seems to have been his father's least favorite son, even though God saw the man he had created David to be and guided Samuel to anoint him as king. As David's story unfolds throughout Scripture, we see a man faced with many more unmet longings and unwanted behaviors. We see him facing further attacks from Saul, who was jealous of David. We see him summoning another man's wife to his bed and arranging for the husband's death. We see him taking many wives and fathering numerous sons in his search for power and control. And through it all, in one family incident after another (the rape of Tamar by her brother Amnon, the killing of Amnon by his brother Absalom, etc.), David's response or failure to respond may have continued and worsened his and his family's dysfunctional patterns.

It's no wonder, then, that Absalom nursed resentment toward his father for years, eventually plotting to seize his father's throne. Absalom gathered an army, engineered his own anointing as king, and marched on Jerusalem.

When David learned of his son's rebellion, he made a tactical retreat out of Jerusalem. David endured one blow after another. He had to send Zadok, his priest and pastor, back to Jerusalem; he discovered that his friend and advisor, Ahithophel, was a traitor; he sent his loyal, aged friend, Hushai, back to Jerusalem; and he was told by Ziba that Saul's grandson, Mephibosheth, to whom David had shown nothing but kindness, was among the conspirators.

That would be a lot for anyone to bear. But it got worse:

As King David approached Bahurim, a man from the same clan as Saul's family came out from there. His name was Shimei son of Gera, and he cursed as he came out. (2 Samuel 16:5)

Remember that Saul was David's predecessor as king. And David was not from Saul's family . . . but Shimei was. So you could call Shimei, in today's terms, a "partisan."

He pelted David and all the king's officials with stones, though all the troops and the special guard were on David's right and left. As he cursed, Shimei said, "Get out, get out, you murderer, you scoundrel! The LORD has repaid you for all the blood you shed in the household of Saul, in whose place you have reigned. The LORD has given the kingdom into the hands of your son Absalom. You have come to ruin because you are a murderer!"

Then Abishai son of Zeruiah said to the king, "Why should this dead dog curse my lord the king? Let me go over and cut off his head."

But the king said, "What does this have to do with you, you sons of Zeruiah? If he is cursing because the LORD said to him, 'Curse David,' who can ask, 'Why do you do this?'"

David then said to Abishai and all his officials, "My son, my own flesh and blood, is trying to kill me. How much more, then, this Benjamite! Leave him alone; let him curse, for the LORD has told him to. It may be that the LORD will look upon my misery and restore to me his covenant blessing instead of his curse today."

So David and his men continued along the road while Shimei was going along the hillside opposite him, cursing as he went and throwing stones at him and showering him with dirt. The king and all the people with him arrived at their destination exhausted. And there he refreshed himself. (2 Samuel 16:6–14)

This had to be one of the lowest points of David's whole life. He'd been wounded by his own father. He'd been hunted by Saul. He'd lived in caves while the king sought his life. He'd mourned his best friend Jonathan's death—and Saul's too. He'd been exposed as an adulterer and murderer. He'd lost a child. But now his own son had betrayed him. His own son sought not only to dethrone him, but to kill him! He'd been driven from his city, separated from his family, betrayed by his closest friends, stripped of his kingly splendor, and exiled from his royal city. And then, to top it off, some sorry protestor comes along and starts throwing rocks and dirt and curses at him.

David's response ("It may be that the LORD will see my distress and repay me with good for the cursing I am receiving today") may seem strange to us, but I think those are the words of a man whose emotional tank is empty. I think like anyone, he longed for acceptance, especially from those closest to him. I imagine that he felt the sting of rejection again and again in his life, and this situation just reinforced the unmet longing that caused that hurt—a hurt that may never have gone away for the rest of his life.

## Attacks and Absences

You may never face an armed rebellion led by your own child, but chances are you've experienced the sting of a longing in your heart and soul that went unmet; it may not have been as severe or sustained as what David suffered, or it may have been even worse. Our unmet longings are scattered throughout the course of our lives, ranging from simply not being invited out to dinner with friends to something as painful as an abusive parent or spouse. Some are rooted in our childhood traumas, of course, and others can have later sources.

Psychologist Arielle Schwartz writes:

> Childhood traumas can range from having faced extreme violence and neglect to having confronted feelings of not belonging, being unwanted, or being chronically misunderstood. You may have grown up in an environment where your curiosity and enthusiasm were constantly devalued. Perhaps you were brought up in a family where your parents had unresolved traumas of their own, which impaired their ability to attend to your emotional needs. Or, you may have faced vicious sexual or physical attacks. In all such situations, you learn to compensate by developing defenses around your most vulnerable parts.[2]

Numerous factors influence how deeply and how long these unmet longings hurt us. We can categorize their sources in two ways. Some come from *attacks*, such as David experienced at the hands of his son; they include name calling and other insults, manipulation, teasing, sexual or physical abuse, and more. Other hurts we feel come from *absences*, such as a parent who leaves—or one who is distant emotionally or physically—as well as from a lack of affirming or loving words, being ignored by friends or family members, being dismissed as unimportant, etc.

Both attacks and absences can hurt deeply. Attacks and absences always leave us with unmet longings, whether fleeting or lasting. A single attack of high intensity, such as being sexually or physically abused, can cause a lifetime of pain. However, so can attacks that are less intense, such as being ridiculed and called names on a childhood playground or being singled out and ostracized for your race or gender. These can also inflict a lifetime of hurt upon our souls.

Similarly, the pain of unmet longings may follow one-time absences of high intensity, such as a parent missing our biggest football game of the year, being stood up by a date, or a parent deserting the family. But enduring or recurring absences, such as a parent being emotionally unengaged, being excluded from important office meetings, or hardly ever feeling affirmed or approved of by significant people in our lives can also leave a deep and lasting wound.

As uniquely created individuals, of course, we all respond to attacks and absences differently. Something that devastates one individual may have little effect on another. I've heard many people say, "I've had a relatively easy life compared to others," but one person's pain never truly compares with another. And ignoring, dismissing, or downplaying the effects of attacks and absences on our own lives may prevent us from dealing with our hurts, healing from them, and moving forward into the best possible future. The diagram on the next page depicts how both attacks and absences can lead to varying levels of pain in our souls. You'll see that both the frequency of a specific type of painful event and the intensity of that painful event directly correlate to the level of pain felt—whether mild, moderate, or extreme.

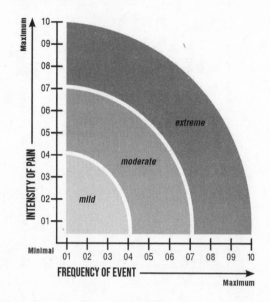

**ATTACKS [Examples]**

Sexual Abuse

Physical Abuse

Bullying

Manipulation/Control

Hurtful Words

**ABSENCES [Examples]**

Disinterest/Disengagement

Abandonment

Emotional/Physical Absence

Lack of Empathy

Lack of Attention

Lack of Loving Words

## When Longings Go Unmet

Just as we respond to attacks and absences differently, so it helps to understand how different unmet longings can look and feel in our lives. Unmet longings may vary, not only according to their intensity and frequency, but also according to their source, as the examples in the following table illustrate.

Author, therapist, and pastor Dr. Ted Roberts has told me often, "You can't change what you don't understand." I completely agree, and I also think it's true that you can't understand what you don't recognize. So, in these next few pages we will attempt to show what it looks like for these seven areas of universal human longings to go unmet, in the hope that you'll recognize yourself and your own longings in some of these situations. The following stories are real-life scenarios; however, names have been changed at times to respect the privacy of the individuals.

## UNMET LONGINGS TABLE

| Longings | Mom / Dad | Siblings / Relatives | Friends | Others |
|---|---|---|---|---|
| **1. Acceptance** | • Dad never said, "I love you"<br>• Mom regularly treated me as weird or different | • My brother teased me for being different<br>• Grandpa never seemed to want to spend time with me | • My best friends often said I was weird | • Teachers valued me based on my grades |
| **2. Appreciation** | • Never heard Mom say "I'm proud of you," or "Great job" | • Often helped my sister clean her room but was never thanked; felt used | • I often cook for my roommates, but they never help me clean up | • My coach often told me to try harder even when I played my best |
| **3. Affection** | • Dad didn't give me hugs or comfort me when I was upset<br>• Mom often didn't pick me up when I wanted to be held | • My brother always seemed to be irritated with me rather than being kind in words and actions | • My best friend is often stand-offish physically and refrains from anything deemed "sappy" or "emotional" | • I told my husband about my difficult day and he just said "that sucks" when I wanted physical affection and comfort |

| | | | | |
|---|---|---|---|---|
| **4. Access** | • Dad was often gone on work trips or at the office<br>• Mom was emotionally distant | • My sister avoided me growing up | • I've spent many Friday nights alone recently without friends | • My boss is seldom there when I need his help |
| **5. Attention** | • Dad never cared too much about my hobbies or interests<br>• Mom never entered my world; said my interests were "silly" | • My grandma never asked me how my games were going or what I enjoyed about sports | • My best friends only want to hang out if we do what they want to do | • My life coach talks about himself all the time rather than seeking to understand me |
| **6. Affirmation of Feelings** | • It was unacceptable to be sad or upset in my family growing up<br>• Mom often told me not to be so whiny | • I recently told my sister how hard my year was and she told me I was partly to blame | • Growing up, my friends often said I was overreacting | • I told my teacher how sad I was about my struggles with math and he said I just wasn't a math person |
| **7. Assurance of Safety** | • My parents lived paycheck-to-paycheck so I grew up worrying about money and my basic needs | • I was picked on and beat up as a kid and my brother never stood up for me | • My best friends teased me quite a bit | • I was sexually abused by a family friend |

## Acceptance

Like Ben, whose memorable experience opened this chapter, Sharon remembers longing for acceptance throughout her childhood and youth; this longing continued into adulthood. She grew up as the middle child in a family of seven, and she always felt different from her siblings. They excelled in sports or academics and won plaudits from Mom and Dad—but Sharon was an average student and a non-athlete. Remarks from family members communicated that they expected little of her. When her high school graduation approached, her parents let her know that she didn't have to enter college but would probably be happier finding a good husband and devoting herself to homemaking. Today, although she earned graduate degrees in a challenging field (in addition to her successful marriage and family life), she continues to struggle with feelings of inadequacy and longs to be accepted and valued for who she is.

## Appreciation

Courtney was speaking at a large work event. She had spent hours preparing and was excited to offer her wisdom to the audience. She was particularly thrilled that her mom was attending the event, as Courtney's mom hadn't heard her daughter speak publicly before. Courtney had a rocky relationship with her mother but was looking forward to having her support. The event went off without a hitch, and Courtney was happy with what she was able to communicate. She knew she'd done a fantastic job, but she felt sad after the event. After a bit of processing with a friend, she realized she was really hoping her mom would say something like, "you did so well" or "I'm proud of you." But her mom had left shortly after the event and went about her evening offering no encouragement, appreciation, or positive feedback. Once again, Courtney was experiencing an unmet longing to feel appreciated by her mom.

## Affection

Mateo and Sofia had been dating for several months and were hanging out one evening after spending the day together. They were getting ready to say goodbye to one another. Mateo was anticipating a quick goodbye and hoped to get a couple things done before turning in for the night. Sofia, on the other hand, was looking for a few minutes of emotional and physical affection. She approached him and gave him a hug, holding on and making eye contact with him. Mateo hugged her but then dropped his arms. Sofia continued to hold on and speak in a soft voice. "I just want to stand here and hug you, and engage with you," she said. Mateo lingered for a few moments longer, but then broke her embrace. "I really have got to get going," he said. Sofia didn't want to be "clingy," but she couldn't help feeling sad in that moment as her longing for affection went unmet.

## Access

Eugene, a second-generation Chinese American, grew up with a mom and dad who provided for his material needs. They put food on the table, took him to church, and encouraged him to work hard at school. His mom took interest in his life, asked about school and his friends, and had a good understanding of him. His dad was physically present, and Eugene saw him most mornings, evenings, and weekends, but he didn't talk much with Eugene. When they did exchange a few words, their conversations usually revolved around working hard in school and getting good grades. To Eugene, his dad seemed to be emotionally inaccessible, off in some distant world, uninterested in the lives of the family, and too busy or preoccupied. When Eugene had a question or expressed a need, his dad seemed inaccessible and unavailable. Eugene longed to know that his father was accessible and there for him, but grew up aware that, in many ways, he wasn't.

## Attention

Rob was an even-tempered, happy kid who loved sports—especially basketball—growing up. His dad, however, didn't take much interest in Rob's hobbies or his internal world. "I only did activities with my dad if it was something he was interested in," Rob told me. "Basically, he'd bring my brothers and me along to go hunting, but besides that he never sought to understand my world." Rob's dad didn't take much interest in his likes, dislikes, opinions, or interests. He felt unknown and misunderstood by his dad. As an adult, Rob's heart sank anytime he talked about this. He is still trying to grow out of the pain of the lack of attention he received from his father as a child.

## Affirmation of Feelings

Raven had just had a tough week at work. She worked over sixty hours, navigated conflicts with coworkers, was criticized by her boss for not completing a few tasks on time, and, to top it off, could hardly sleep. Friday had finally arrived, and Raven was texting her friend Sara about the difficulties. Sara replied, "Well why don't I come by tonight and bring some tea, and we can chat." Raven anticipated seeing her friend and unloading her burdens. Later that evening Sara showed up, and the two hung out for several hours. During their time together, Raven mentioned how she was so glad the week was over. Rather than engaging with Raven, asking questions, or empathizing, Sara talked at length about how bad her own week had been. At first Raven tried to respond, but when Sara continued without a break, Raven just let her talk. Raven got quieter as the evening went on. She had longed for a listening ear and a friend who would affirm her feelings, without judgment. But instead Raven felt unseen and unheard. She went to bed that night with unmet longings for confirmation, validation, and affirmation of her feelings.

## Assurance of Safety

Ivan was adopted from Asia when he was two years old by a Caucasian family in the United States. He grew up in a rural area of the country and was one of the few Asian kids around. In elementary school, he began to be picked on and bullied because he was different. Most days Ivan feared for his safety. He desperately wanted someone to intervene and protect him. He longed to be protected and provided for physically and emotionally. He not only wanted to be loved for who he was; he wanted to know that he could go to school and walk around his neighborhood without fear. But no one protected him. No one stood up for him. No one prevented him from being pushed around, and he carried that insecurity into adulthood. Even today Ivan longs for a sense of the assurance of safety.

# The Pain and the Thirst

Our unmet longings, especially if they are consistent, can lead to deeply rooted pain in our lives, causing an insatiable thirst to have our longings fulfilled. Often, unmet longings that are rooted in our past and then experienced again in our current situations can create a potent and devastating mixture of emotions, since they bring with them all the pain of our previous experiences mixed with recent reinforcement and new hurts.

When I pulled up to my friends on my skateboard as a fifteen-year-old, I experienced rejection rather than the acceptance I longed for. I felt not only the disapproval of my friends in that moment, but also the renewal of that unmet need which I had endured for years. This situation triggered past experiences where statements like "You're not good enough," "Something is wrong with you," "You don't fit in this family," and "You don't belong" were communicated to me. When our longings go unmet in the present, they reinforce the hurts we've sustained and the lies we've learned and believed in the past.

When Courtney finished speaking at her work event and didn't receive what she hoped to hear—her mother's appreciation and approval—it reinforced her feeling of not measuring up to her mom's expectations. Instead of starting to heal a wound from her past, it opened the wound again. She felt incapable, inadequate, and incompetent. The unmet longing of appreciation had developed a deep cavern in her soul, and this longing once again, after the event, confirmed to her what had always been communicated by attacks and absences in her past.

In Ivan's case, since he had been bullied and beaten for the color of his skin growing up, he hesitated to open up and trust me when we first met. He wondered if I (Ben) was safe. Would I, too, bully him for being Asian? Would I confirm what he believed to be true: *people aren't safe; you can't trust them; they'll harm you physically and emotionally?* Over time, Ivan began to experience that I was a safe person. As we became closer, Ivan's longing for the assurance of safety began to be met. He started to change, relaxing and opening up to other people. He grew less anxious and angry. He started to see Jesus meet the unmet longings of his heart and grow him through relationships with other safe people. Within a few weeks, Ivan said that I was only the second man he had ever trusted.

We all experience attacks and absences throughout our lives. The Bible is full of examples of this reality, for both the Christian and non-Christian alike. Being a Christian does not mean we will escape these attacks, absences, and unmet longings. Joseph was betrayed by his brothers and sold into slavery (Genesis 37). Potiphar was lied to by his wife and Joseph was lied about (Genesis 39). Noah and his family faced the flood and the uprooting of their lives (Genesis 7). Moses was abandoned by his parents as an infant (Exodus 2). Tamar was raped by her brother (2 Samuel 13). The woman at the well in John 4 was accustomed to being treated as less than others because of her race and her past. Jesus himself was publicly mocked, tortured, stripped naked, and killed unjustly for crimes he didn't commit.

One of the greatest tragedies in life is that the Enemy uses these attacks, absences, and unmet longings to breed shame in our lives. Shame says, "I am bad" or "there's something wrong with me." Shame is the faulty core belief that something is inherently wrong with our identity. We can take on shame as the lens through which we see ourselves and the world around us, and this prevents us from living into the potential and purpose God intends for us. It also hinders our ability to positively influence the lives of others around us. When we leave our shame and the causes of it unaddressed, we perpetuate the destructive cycle of causing other people to also experience shame.

In her book, *Unashamed*, Christine Caine says:

> When shame has been pumping through a heart, over time the heart itself grows toxic. When we are wounded, we leak toxic waste, and that waste poisons us and the people around us—even when we are completely unaware of it. . . . The reality is:
>
> - Hurt people hurt people.
> - Broken people break people.
> - Shattered people shatter people.
> - Damaged people damage people.
> - Wounded people wound people.
> - Bound people bind people.[3]

## Read Your Own Life

The pain caused by our unmet needs—legitimate needs, God-given needs—can be devastating. It might prompt us to wonder where God was, where he is, and why he let such things happen. We can wonder if he actually cares and if he has anything to say to us in our struggles. And we are not alone in such moments. Even King David, as he grieved his son's rebellion and faced one of the darkest moments of his life, cried out in what became the Bible's Psalm 3:

> LORD, how many are my foes!
>     How many rise up against me!
> Many are saying of me,
>     "God will not deliver him."
>
> But you, LORD, are a shield around me,
>     my glory, the One who lifts my head high.
> I call out to the LORD,
>     and he answers me from his holy mountain.
>
> I lie down and sleep;
>     I wake again, because the LORD sustains me.
> I will not fear though tens of thousands
>     assail me on every side.
>
> Arise, LORD!
>     Deliver me, my God!
> Strike all my enemies on the jaw;
>     break the teeth of the wicked.
>
> From the LORD comes deliverance.
>     May your blessing be on your people. (Psalm 3:1–8)

The effects of our unmet needs, the results of attacks and absences in our lives, can feel unbearable at times—but our stories aren't over. God mourns and cries with us (John 11:35). He is close to the brokenhearted. God never wastes our pain and suffering if we allow him to use it. He promises to use even our darkest chapters to bring resolution to our stories and make us more like himself (Romans 8:28–29). He never uses our past to shame us but will use it to shape us. He promises to develop endurance, character, and hope in us (Romans 5:3–5). He promises to restore us and make us strong and steadfast (1 Peter 5:10), bringing us more and more into lives of wholeness.

Whatever pain, hurt, and unmet longings we experience, we can take heart because Jesus has already overcome the world. Our battles are temporary, and one day when we see Jesus face to face, in a place even greater than Eden, it will outweigh every unmet longing.

> For our light and momentary troubles are achieving for us an eternal glory that far outweighs them all. So we fix our eyes not on what is seen, but on what is unseen, since what is seen is temporary, but what is unseen is eternal. (2 Corinthians 4:17–18)

Like the Apostle Paul, who after being shipwrecked, stoned, imprisoned, and beaten, said he had learned "the secret of being content in any and every situation," we too can be content, knowing that Jesus is with us, comforts us, and has prepared a place for us with him forever in eternity (Philippians 4:12). We can know that we can make it through and bear all things through Christ who strengthens us (Philippians 4:13). No matter our past, we know our Healer. No matter our storm, we know our Anchor. No matter our circumstances, we know our Future.

Jesus desires to set us free from the effects of these attacks and absences and fulfill our unmet longings. He desires to bring healing and transformation. We can rest assured that Jesus cares, because he says he came for the sick, not the healthy (Mark 2:17); he came to heal the brokenhearted and bind up their wounds (Psalm 147:3); he came to set the captives free (Luke 4:18); he came so that we may have life to the full, here and now (John 10:10). He will one day make all things new and wipe away every tear from our eyes (Revelation 21:4) as we enjoy an intimate relationship with him in a place that is even greater than Eden (Revelation 21:1–3). He came to bind up and heal our wounds, but we must understand what those wounds are so that we can take them to him and invite him to heal them. As author and therapist Dr. Dan Allender says, "Take seriously the story that God has given you to live. It's time to read your own life, because your story is the one that could set us all ablaze."[4]

As hard as it is to look carefully at our unmet longings, we must do so if we want to heal and grow. To quote Henry Cloud:

> Although suffering is negative, it is part of life—especially the growth part of life. No one grows to maturity who does not understand suffering. For example, dealing with our hurts, sins, and failures involves pain, both within us and in our relationships with others.[5]

We cannot heal or grow in isolation. So be brave. Identify your unmet longings from the past and in the present and think through the ways your longings have gone—or are currently going—unmet. Take seriously the story you have, the things you have weathered, what you have overcome. Begin now to process your past and present with Jesus and with safe, trustworthy people. We need to allow Jesus and others to speak into our lives, support us, and encourage us in our journey. As you do this, experiencing more and more of the thriving life God desires for you, be prepared for God to use you to bring healing and change to others. (He rarely does something through us before he does something in us.)

Finally, after reviewing the Questions for Reflection, take some time to work through the "Depth of Longings Assessment" on the following pages; it will help to lay the groundwork for the work you and God will do together in the coming chapters.

↗ **DEPTH OF LONGINGS ASSESSMENT** ↗

This assessment, developed in collaboration with Dr. Ted Roberts, is intended to help you identify and understand the unmet longings that have been holding you back in your journey toward wholeness. Please check item under Y (for "Yes") or N (for "No").

Y   N

___ ___ I have trouble stopping certain actions even though they are unhelpful/destructive

___ ___ I repeat destructive behaviors over and over, starting early in my life

___ ___ I often have increased sexual desires when I am lonely

___ ___ I feel loyal to people even though they have hurt me

___ ___ I use the internet, streaming media, eating, and hobbies as a way to check out

___ ___ I repeatedly put off certain tasks

___ ___ I feel badly about myself because of shameful experiences in my past

___ ___ I hide some of my behaviors from others

___ ___ After engaging in an unwanted behavior, I feel sad afterward

___ ___ I feel controlled at times by my unwanted behaviors

___ ___ I fear the rejection of other people

___ ___ I think what I do is never good enough

___ ___ I feel I'm not worthy of love

___ ___ I fear that I am a bother to people

___ ___ I feel unknown and misunderstood

___ ___ I believe that my thoughts and opinions don't matter

___ ___ I have fears about my safety, finances, or emotional needs

## Scoring

Count how many statements to which you answered "Yes."

Total "Yes" Responses ___

*A score of 6 or more "Yes" responses indicates significant longings may have gone unmet in both the past and present. We recommend finding a professional therapist to help you navigate these unresolved areas of unmet longings and pain. This assessment is not conclusive, but rather meant to be an indication of the depths of unmet longings and hurt in your life.*

# Questions for Reflection

1. Of the Seven Longings we've discussed in this book, which would you say are the two you find yourself thinking about or desiring most?
2. In what ways have these two longings gone unmet in the past year? Throughout life growing up?
3. Can you identify moments when these longings went unmet through attacks? Absences?
4. Try praying this prayer of David before you complete the "Depth of Longings Assessment":

> Search me, God, and know my heart;
>> test me and know my anxious thoughts.
> See if there is any offensive way in me,
>> and lead me in the way everlasting.
> (Psalm 139:23–24)

# CHAPTER FOUR

# IDENTIFYING THE UNWANTED

Some things are easier to understand than other things.

Why do you wear your favorite jeans so often? Easy; because you like how they feel and look.

Why do you take the same route to work nearly every day? Again, easy; because it's usually the quickest way to go . . . and also has a convenient coffee shop drive-through.

Why do you listen to Ke$ha's music? There's no good reason for that.

Okay, but seriously, it's easy to understand why we do harmless or constructive things. But it's much harder to fathom the reasons behind our unwanted behaviors and destructive tendencies. Why do we lash out at people we love? Why do we eat compulsively or indulge in pornography? Why do we have toxic thoughts about ourselves and others? Or indulge in other habits that we don't like—even hate—but nonetheless turn to again and again?

## Longing for Connection

I (Ben) grew up in Virginia, with brief stints in Thailand and the Philippines (my parents were in full-time Christian ministry).

Much in my childhood would have seemed idyllic to most boys, at least on the surface: traveling the world, vacations at tropical beaches, making all kinds of friends, and parents who stayed together and provided financially. But events beyond my control planted the seeds of unwanted behaviors that I wouldn't fully understand until many years later. I was surrounded by Christianity. My parents worked for a Christian organization. I grew up going to a church that talked about Jesus and the importance of knowing him personally. I knew at an early age that God wanted a personal relationship with me, and that I had done wrong things and was separated from God, but that through Jesus's life, death, and resurrection I could obtain forgiveness and a reconciled relationship with God. I gave my life to this cause at an early age, and while my relationship with God was restored, other relationships were broken.

My father worked long hours at the office and traveled for weeks at a time on ministry trips. I felt his physical distance, but things didn't seem much better when he was home. He was quick to get angry and yell at me when I misbehaved. His anger was explosive. I constantly felt like I couldn't measure up to his expectations. I wasn't told why things were wrong; I just had to obey. I could never explain myself because it was seen as "talking back." I longed to be understood. I remember repeatedly getting in trouble and being spanked while my dad was in a state of rage. It was terrifying. I lived in fear of my father for years.

At the age of eight, I began reacting to those painful realities. I would respond angrily to my dad, lashing out in an attempt to protect myself from hurt. I developed anxiety and was always on alert, anticipating the next time I would experience rejection. I turned inward, accepting the lies that others were communicating about my value and experiencing depression because of it. I grasped for control, developing Obsessive Compulsive Disorder as a response to the chaos that surrounded me. I escaped and medicated myself with overeating. And when things felt unbearable, suicidal thoughts entered in.

I continued looking for something more to cope with the painful realities I was experiencing. I soon found something that could give me a high like a drug, and it was free: hardcore pornography. I didn't go looking for it; my friends in middle school introduced me to it (I later learned that this is the case with most kids who are exposed to pornography). My friends put it on the TV, and I was shocked and disgusted, so I left the room. But curiosity brought me back, and I was soon hooked.

I began seeking out porn in the months to come, and eventually became addicted. I knew it was wrong, but I couldn't stop. I was torn. I loved the escape it provided and the endless amounts of pseudo-acceptance and attention I could get from the women on the screen. For a moment in time, it was as if I was the object of their affection. Yet I felt immense shame after viewing it and made countless promises to God to stop. I hated what I was doing and began to hate myself. Porn began to damage my relationships with my friends as I began to isolate from them due to the shame I was experiencing, and I struggled to view my female friends as more than just objects of my own sexual gratification. I felt immense distance in my relationship with Jesus as I sinned against him time after time.

My use of porn intensified throughout middle school and high school. My mental health issues got worse, and my dad became even more distant. He started abusing alcohol. I can remember weeks at a time when he and I didn't speak. I resented him for his anger and distance, along with the worthlessness I felt as a result.

I began to believe that those who were supposed to be there for me would let me down and reject me. I had an agonizing sense that something was wrong with me—that I was the problem. If I were different, people wouldn't reject me. If I were better, I would be worth something. I didn't know who I was or how much I was valued. I felt like a burden to those around me—especially my family. Deep down, I longed for two things—acceptance and attention. I wanted to be valued and loved for who I was, and I longed to be known and understood. I tried to find someone or something to meet these needs as I jumped from one group of friends to another. I found a group temporarily, but the fulfillment of these needs was fleeting. It seemed as though in one season I was the most popular kid around, and in the next I was the one everyone made fun of.

This vicious cycle continued as I sank deeper into unwanted behaviors, thinking all along that my struggles with porn, anger, and mental health issues were my unique problems. I soon realized they were just my attempted solutions.

## Futility and Failure

As a boy I had a legitimate need, a longing for attention, especially from those closest and most important to me. When this longing was frustrated, I felt rejected, neglected, and misunderstood. So I tried to cope with those feelings—by lashing out in anger, by seeking popularity in the hope that others would notice me and know me, and by consuming pornography.

I soon found myself stuck in the cycle that the first-century writer Paul described: "I do not understand what I do. For what I want to do I do not do, but what I hate I do" (Romans 7:15).

Can you identify with that sentiment? That frustration? Have you found yourself struggling with unwanted behaviors and not knowing why? Maybe you've tried to address some unhealthy choices—such as abusing drugs or alcohol, binge eating, or over-spending—by simply "trying harder to do better."

Many of our unwanted behaviors are what the Bible calls sin. At the core, sin is wrong because it goes against God's charac-ter. It goes against his honesty, righteousness, love, and truth. It hurts God, ourselves, and others. It leads to disconnection and alienation. Whatever your story is and whatever unwanted behaviors you turn to, it is important to know that there is more behind your sin than the nature all humans are born with. "In the biblical perspective, sin is not only an act of wrongdoing but a state of alienation from God."[1] We have all sinned, done wrong, and found ourselves in a state of alienation from God. Have your unwanted behaviors left you experiencing a sense of separation from God? Are you feeling like God is distant and waiting for you to get your act together before he shows up? Have you felt stuck, experiencing feelings of frustration at everything you have tried without much movement or lasting change?

I was stuck for over half of my lifetime in unwanted behaviors that had more of a grip on me as time went on. What were initially occasional behaviors shifted into compulsive patterns that eventually started looking and feeling like addictions. I found myself unable to stop, no matter how much I wanted to. I started doubting God's power and promises because I certainly wasn't experiencing any of the abundant life and freedom the Bible describes. I tried everything I knew to do but remained stuck.

If you are looking for a breakthrough and people who can relate with you in your unwanted behavior, look at Paul's words to the church in Ephesus, where Paul invites and urges his friends to listen and walk in the life of God as individuals and a community:

> So I tell you this, and insist on it in the Lord, that you must no longer live as the Gentiles do, in the futility of their thinking. They are darkened in their understanding and separated from the life of God because of the ignorance that is in them due to the hardening of their hearts. Having lost all sensitivity, they have given themselves over to sensuality so as to indulge in every kind of impurity, and they are full of greed.
>
> That, however, is not the way of life you learned when you heard about Christ and were taught in him in accordance with the truth that is in Jesus. You were taught, with regard to your former way of life, to put off your old self, which is being corrupted by its deceitful desires; to be made new in the attitude of your minds; and to put on the new self, created to be like God in true righteousness and holiness. (Ephesians 4:17–24)

Paul shows us the progression of any unwanted behavior or sin in our lives. He was writing to believers in Jesus Christ, but he compared their state to that of non-Christians. It's a mistake to think that if people come to faith, they're immune to unwanted behaviors and compulsive patterns. True, when someone becomes a Christian, that person is reconnected with God, but Paul's words suggest that a Christian can be in Christ and yet "separated from the life of God"—separated from the goodness, closeness, and satisfaction that a close personal relationship with God brings. This is the life of God, the life he intended for us to experience in the Garden of Eden which we were designed for. He says, "I'll tell you this and insist on it in the Lord, that you must no longer live as the Gentiles do." His comparison of the "Gentile" ways of life with the way of Jesus reveals that there is the possibility for a Christian to return to former ways of living.

Paul describes this old way of life as one of being "separated from the life of God," being "darkened in their understanding," experiencing a "hardening of their hearts" with a loss of "sensitivity." He sums up this former way of living as "futility in their thinking." Could it be that there are ways, in our lives, in which we also get caught up in this old, futile cycle? That we experience disconnection from the life of God and therefore experience unmet longings, growing darkened in our understanding as we believe lie after lie about God, ourselves, and others? That we develop a loss of sensitivity as we numb our pain by indulging in unwanted behaviors?

I have witnessed countless ways this cycle has played out in my own life and in the lives of many others I've led through healing groups over the years. It often goes like this: an individual is disconnected from the life of God—their Seven Longings go unmet by others growing up, they begin to get caught in futile thinking, and they start believing lies driven by the hurt of their unmet longings about God, about themselves, and about others. They think they have to hide, and they feel so much shame.

They make futile commitments to try harder to overcome their unwanted behaviors. They return again and again to those unwanted behaviors and become darkened in their understanding, losing hope, losing a sense of reality, and experiencing further shame and isolation. This only serves to perpetuate the feelings of unmet longings and cravings for unwanted behaviors, becoming a downward spiral leading to a loss of sensitivity (or numbness), a lack of hope, and increasingly unhealthy choices.

Another example of futile thinking is the ways many of us have tried to overcome unwanted behaviors. One of those ways is what many call "accountability," an approach that can often focus on rules and restrictions as a way to change behaviors.

During my college years, I met with a friend once a week to talk about my struggle with pornography. Each of us would share if we had looked at porn (and how often) during the week. Week after week, we committed to trying harder the next week. We came up with ideas to stop our unwanted behavior, like going to bed earlier, leaving our computers in common areas, and so on. We were focused on the behavior rather than why we turned to pornography. This aligned with the model of accountability taught by many Christians: make commitments, agree to rules, and accept punishments or further restrictions if you falter or fail—all in an attempt to keep a safe distance from temptation and sin. I tried everything I knew to stop going back to porn. I soon felt just like Paul when he wrote about the legalistic Christians in the first-century Colossian church: "These rules may seem wise because they require strong devotion, pious self-denial, and severe bodily discipline. But they provide no help in conquering a person's evil desires" (Colossians 2:23 NLT).

Don't get me wrong, there is wisdom in avoiding our destructive behaviors and we definitely need support from others to grow. But the accountability model that many of us have tried is futile because it is rule-based and focuses on modifying a behavior, which will in time lead to a greater sense of alienation. Have you ever felt that way? Have you noticed that the ways you have tried to get unstuck have left you feeling more stuck, separated, and disconnected from the life of God?

Maybe your unmet longings, unwanted behaviors, and futile attempts to change your behaviors have left you feeling even more numb. Paul goes on to unpack this reality in Ephesians 4:19, saying, "Having lost all sensitivity." The word "sensitivity" can also mean "feeling." In other words, the "life of God"—which includes connection, vulnerability, and all the things that are healthy and restorative—is lost. We lose all sense of the wholeness we crave. We lose the fulfillment of the Seven Longings intended to be satisfied by God, self, and others, along with the thriving and abundant life for which we were all created. Separation from this "life of God" leads only to lifelessness and pain. We lose touch with vulnerability. We can't feel our feelings. We feel numb.

Though Paul doesn't use the words "unwanted behaviors," his description seems apt for someone with compulsive, unhealthy patterns. What does a stuck person do when something triggers those behaviors? Instead of feeling and working through the woundedness and pain, they "having lost sensitivity . . . give themselves over to sensuality." They trade in lasting feeling for fleeting touch.

It's a horrible trade-off. It's not a trade any healthy person would willingly or knowingly make. But when we're accustomed to futile thinking, darkened understanding, and hardening hearts, our numbness and apathy leads not to spirituality but to sensuality. One commentator writes, "If verse 18 traces the problem back to its origin, verse 19 shows its outcome. 'Insensitivity' in one direction leads to 'sensuality' in another."[2] In the words of C. S. Lewis, we pursue "spoiled goods"[3] and cheap imitations. "Badness is only spoiled goodness," Lewis wrote. "And there must be something good first before it can be spoiled."[4] Sexuality and sensuality were designed by God; they are good and precious gifts when pursued in the ways he designed. But the sensuality that springs from futile thinking, darkened understanding, and hardened hearts serves up "badness" rather than goodness into the lives of those consuming it.

Paul doesn't use the word "coping" in the above passage, but the idea can be concluded from his line of thought. This is not healthy coping, however; it is unhealthy coping. Mark and Debbie Laaser describe unhealthy coping as "the way we avoid or numb the painful feelings, finding ways to comfort or protect ourselves when we are hurting. . . . Unhealthy coping is a false solution in that we hope the coping strategies will work, but they never do."[5] Trying to meet legitimate needs in illegitimate ways will never work, whether we try them as individuals or in relationships with others.

## Unhealthy Attempts to Cope

My friend, therapist Jay Stringer, has done a lot of work and research on unwanted behaviors, which he defines as any behavior that, at the end of the day, we wish was not a part of our lives. Similarly, we define unwanted behaviors as any compulsive thought, belief, or action you want to stop but can't.

You may have unmet longings in your life that contribute to some unwanted behaviors. Perhaps you've thought, "People aren't safe, and they will reject me," and you can't seem to shake it. Maybe you harbor a belief that you are not loveable, despite what others tell you. Perhaps you're like 46 percent of Americans who report feeling alone, or like the 47 percent who feel left out.[6] Or maybe you struggle with consistent obsessive thoughts or actions about money, your appearance, or material things. Maybe you battle depression.

You may have tried different ways of coping with lingering hurts springing from unmet needs. Maybe you try to cope with your uncomfortable emotions by overeating or smoking weed. Perhaps you immerse yourself in TV watching to numb your pain.[7] Maybe you spend money you don't have or go on shopping sprees to distract you from facing the hard-to-deal-with emotions.

Maybe you're among the 91–99 percent of men and 62–90 percent of women who turn to pornography.[8] The following is a list of common unwanted behaviors we can get stuck in. Can you identify any coping behaviors that hold you back from the life of wholeness God has for you?

## COPING BEHAVIOR TABLE

| Adultery | Alcohol(ism) | Anger/Rage |
|---|---|---|
| Anxiety/Fear/Worry | Approval of Others | Boasting/Bragging |
| Body Image Issues | Cheating/Cutting Corners | Complaining |
| Control | Depression | Disobedience/Rebellion |
| Divorce/Separation | Drugs/Substance Abuse/Pills | Fantasy |
| Fear of Failure | Fear of Intimacy | Gambling |
| Greed | Hopelessness | Insecurity |
| Isolation/Withdrawal | Jealousy/Envy | Lack of Growth |
| Laziness | Lying/Deceit/Dishonesty | Materialism |
| Overeating/Undereating | Oversleeping/Undersleeping | Overspending |
| Overworking | Perfectionism | Poor Boundaries |
| Pornography/Arousing Images or Writing | Pride/Self-Righteousness/Judgmentalism | Procrastination |
| Profanity/Swearing/Cursing | Racism | Resentment/Bitterness |
| Self-Harm/Cutting | Self-Sabotage | Self-Worth/Too High or Too Low |
| Sexual Compulsivity | Smoking/Dipping/Vaping | Social Media |

| Stealing | Streaming Media (Netflix, YouTube, etc.) | Suicidal Thoughts |
|---|---|---|
| Unforgiveness | Unhealthy Relationships | Victim Mentality |
| Video Games | | **Total:** |

Do you want to take the next step toward thriving and wholeness? If so, grab a pen and find a quiet spot, silence your devices, and spend some time looking over the list above, circling any of the behaviors on the list that you have struggled with in your lifetime. Be as honest and as thorough as you can be; as my father often said, "A problem well-stated is a problem half-solved."[9] The more honest and thorough you can be, the healthier you will become as you begin to confront your unwanted behaviors and prayerfully consider through the rest of this book the unmet needs they may reveal—and the life-changing steps toward being free to thrive.

## Unhealthy Coping in Relationships

We all have unwanted behaviors. They often start small and unknown to us but grow and get worse over time. In times of high stress, you may find that your unwanted behaviors multiply and intensify. Now that you've defined and identified your unwanted behaviors, it's time to look at how you tend to cope in your relationships with others. Author and therapist Virginia Satir suggests a few ways of coping in relationships.[10] She calls them "Stances" we take in relation to others. All of our relationships, especially our closest ones, are based on love and trust. When something happens in a relationship that makes us question that love and trust, we will normally react in one of the following ways:

## 🎁 The Pleaser Stance

The Pleaser does whatever it takes to keep others happy, to keep judgment and anger at bay, and to prevent other people from leaving. The Pleaser will typically serve, care, and show compassion to the point of burnout. The Pleaser operates from the belief, "It's my fault. I don't matter. I'm not lovable anyway, so what does it matter?" This person knows the needs of others, but stifles personal needs in order to care for others at his or her expense.

## ☞ The Blamer Stance

The Blamer discounts others and thinks only about himself or herself and his or her own context. The Blamer offers many excuses for his or her conduct but won't listen to or accept others' excuses. Assertive and defensive, Blamers will point fingers at others, pouring out anger, judgment, and shame on other people, especially those in the Pleaser Stance.

## 🚫 The Reasoner Stance

This person feels like all logic and no heart. This person will avoid emotion and try to deny or discount the emotions of others. He or she will employ reason and intellect to try to vindicate himself or herself, prove another person wrong, and win the argument—and the Reasoner will almost always win. This person will even use the Bible as a tool or weapon to prove someone else wrong. As this person wins the argument, he or she loses the ability to listen to the heart of the other. Disconnection results.

## 🚫 The Withdrawer Stance

This person strikes an apathetic stance, convinced that the deeper stress-filled issues in life are better avoided rather than engaged. This person will not express an opinion or take a position so as to avoid disagreements. A descent into this stance may happen gradually, perhaps having started in one of the other stances. However, he or she has now reached the limit, shrugs, and says, "Whatever. I don't even care anymore. Do what you want."

As you've read these descriptions, faces and situations may have come to mind that fit into the four stances. But the point, of course, is to help us identify stances that we tend to take and to recognize how none of the above stances promote effective communication. We take these stances because we are seeking to have our longings met. Pleasers may desperately fear not having affection or attention, so they do whatever it takes to please other people and keep them around. Blamers may fear rejection and crave acceptance, so they blame others in order to shift the focus of a problem to them. Those who are operating from the Reasoner Stance may want to feel appreciated, so they try to convince others of the rightness of their position so that people will thank and praise them. People taking the Withdrawer Stance may want to feel safe, so they avoid conflict at all costs. All of these stances are a hindrance to communication, a barrier to feeling heard and understood. Rather than satisfying our longings, they push others farther away and lead to a deepening of unfulfilled longings.

Instead of taking these unhealthy stances, we are designed to live from a place of wholeness and security in who God has made us. We are designed to be secure, knowing how much we are already accepted, affirmed, and safe. This takes practice, but regularly reminding ourselves of all the ways God meets our Seven Longings frees us to give of ourselves in relationships, to be okay when our longings briefly go unmet, and to live from a place of peace. Identifying your "go-to" stance is a crucial step in avoiding misunderstanding and preventing unwanted behaviors in the future.

## Putting Off and Putting On

The progression of unwanted behaviors that Paul depicted in Ephesians 4 may overlap with some of the items you circled in the list on pages 68–69. It's a progression that ends in a kind of disconnection that negatively affects the deepest part of the human heart. Paul's reference to "sensuality" and "every kind of impurity" covers many vices and sins but seems to emphasize sexual sin. Sexual sin can be understood as any thought or action that is outside of God's design for a healthy sexual relationship. This progression ends not with satisfaction and thriving, but with the continual lust for more.

Ephesians 4:17–19 is a map of an unwanted-behavior-riddled life. In Ben's case, the descent into sensuality via pornography created a continual lust for more. How long is it after someone uses porn to medicate a hurting heart and mind before another fix is needed? It never ends. Pornography can't fill the vacuum that happens when a person is "separated from the life of God." As C. S. Lewis said, "If I find in myself a desire which no experience in this world can satisfy, the most probable explanation is that I was made for another world."[11] The God-given longings in everyone will cry out for more until we reconnect with Jesus, his people, and the life he offers that is lived and empowered by all God has given to help us thrive in this life.

The progression starts in verse 17 with Paul's invitation. He appeals to them and urges them to live differently. In verse 18 he clearly states the problem that results from not living differently than the Gentiles. He finally concludes with the outcome in verse 19. From invitation to problem to outcome, Paul's goal is to invite those who are disconnected from the life of God to reconnect to where true life, rather than a never-ending lust for more, is found. If your unwanted behaviors have left you thinking, "Maybe just one more time," or you feel empty or numb with an unquenchable thirst for more, there is hope. How do you move from a place of "never enough" and "always wanting more" to a place of true satisfaction and constant thriving? It is possible, according to Paul; the next verses tell us how.

If you want to begin this process, Paul says, you must "put off the old" (verse 22), and "put on the new" (verse 24). "Putting off the old" includes identifying your unmet longings, your unwanted behaviors, and the things that disconnect you from the life you're meant to lead, and seeing that those things bring disconnection rather than connection to "the life of God." Putting on the new includes learning how we have developed futile ways of thinking and been darkened in our understanding. It includes finding the fulfillment of our longings in healthy ways. We must cease the cycle we have been stuck in and walk backward through the model Paul lays out in Ephesians 4:17–19.

We cannot reconnect with life any other way than by reconnecting with the "life of God," which is relational at its core. There is no long-term solution that is not relational. You cannot do it alone. You were not meant to. This can be a painful start to a beautiful process, but one writer states, "Only in facing the painful truth about ourselves is there hope for healing."[12] Take the first step into hope and healing. Open your arms and embrace reality, so you can begin to grow into who God has made you to be. Write down your unwanted behaviors. Identify (or estimate) when they began. Share the list with a trusted friend, ideally someone who will support you in prayer. And take the time to answer the following questions. You cannot change what you do not know, so get to know the unwanted behaviors you practice, both as an individual and in relationship to others. Doing so will move you closer and closer to a thriving life.

## Questions for Reflection

1. What was the total number of individual coping behaviors from the chart that you have struggled with?
2. What stance(s) have you found yourself occupying in relationships with others?
3. What are your top three unwanted behaviors that you still struggle with, and when did each behavior begin in your life?
4. In relationships, what effect does the stance(s) you take have on you and the other person (or people)?

# LISTEN TO YOUR LONGINGS

I mentioned in this book's introduction how I (Josh) began meeting with Dr. Henry Cloud for counseling years ago, and described some of the ways he helped me identify and understand the unmet longings that were driving my unwanted behaviors, leading to over-commitment and exhaustion. In short, I had become a compulsive rescuer.

Henry helped me to understand that as a child of an alcoholic father, I developed the tendency early in life to rescue others. I grew up feeling like it was my responsibility to hold the family together. When my father became physically and verbally violent toward my mom, I took him on to protect her. There were many times, I believe, that she would have ended up dead had I not intervened. My mom would complain about her problems with my father, and I carried the burden of her emotional distress. I often felt caught in the middle between my mom and dad's problems. Because my father was absent emotionally, it was up to me to comfort her when she was upset.

My sister was fifteen years older than I. She lived down the road with her passive and quiet husband. My dad would often drive down the road to her house and become verbally violent toward her. As a young boy I tried to prevent my dad from hurting her and would often go over there to comfort my sister after my dad had come and gone. In these and other ways, I learned to rescue people as a kid, taking on things that weren't mine to own.

Rescuing loved ones seemed to be one of the few ways I could gain the acceptance and love of my family. I felt valued when I could help my mom with chores around the house, knowing that my dad was often too drunk or too disengaged to help her. I felt like I belonged when I became the man of the house and my mom looked to me for emotional support instead of to my dad. I felt like I had purpose when I could protect my sister and comfort her emotionally.

This rescuing behavior continued into my adult life, leaving me feeling like all of the problems in the world were mine to solve. Henry helped me to see that behind my compulsive desire to rescue others was an unmet longing for acceptance. I wanted to be included, loved, and approved of as I was, no matter what. And there was nothing wrong with that longing; God wanted the same for me—he created me with that longing. But over many years I had tried to meet that need in unhealthy ways—ways that were destroying my life. I was addicted to rescuing people from their problems in an attempt to get acceptance from them and from others. This often left me feeling used and, subsequently, angry at people. Although rescuing gave me a temporary sense of value and a counterfeit version of the acceptance God longed for me to experience, in many ways I was only as emotionally mature as that wounded little boy even though I was well into my fifties. I had not healed and grown beyond that way of functioning; my emotional growth was stunted. I hadn't dealt with that unresolved area of my story, and it was inhibiting my relationship with God, myself, and others.

Peter Scazzero in his book, *Emotionally Healthy Spirituality*, says, "Emotional health and spiritual maturity are inseparable. It is not possible to be spiritually mature while remaining emotionally immature."[1] Another friend, Dr. James Reeves, says, "Your level of emotional maturity will always create a ceiling for your spiritual maturity."[2]

I was a living example of this reality. Though I had a theological degree, had written books, was leading a global ministry, and reached millions yearly, my own spiritual growth was hindered. On the outside I may have looked like one of the most spiritually mature Christian leaders around. But our spiritual maturity isn't determined by our level of knowledge about God, nor by the number of good things we do or how much we pray, read the Bible, serve, or go to church. Spiritual maturity is determined by the level to which we love God, ourselves, and others—the level to which we have been matured by God into Christ-likeness.

My unmet longings and unresolved hurts from the past fueled unwanted behaviors and sin in my life, which hindered my intimacy with God and others. Just as sin against a brother or sister in Christ causes emotional distance until it is reconciled, so my sin was grieving God and hindering my intimacy with him. It wasn't him creating the distance; I was moving away from him every time I defaulted to anger, control, and grasping for the acceptance of others. Although I thought I was loving people by rescuing them from their problems, I was frequently sinning against them because I was enabling them.

## Boulders and Backpacks

The Bible says, "Carry each other's burdens, and in this way you will fulfill the law of Christ. . . . for each one should carry their own load" (Galatians 6:2, 5). On a first reading, this passage can seem confusing. But closer investigation reveals a wealth of wisdom.

The Greek word for "burden" evokes a picture of a person carrying something large and weighty, like a boulder. It suggests something you can't carry alone, something you aren't meant to carry alone. But the Greek word for "load" is different; it's more like an image of someone wearing a backpack. The distinction is important. All of us face burdens at times that we can't possibly carry on our own; we need others to come alongside us and help us. But each of us should carry his or her own load; to avoid responsibility and fail or refuse to do what we can and should do—and expect or allow others to take responsibility from us—is detrimental and destructive to us and to those who think they are helping us.

In my case, my rescuing behavior was like me taking on people's backpacks, preventing them from owning their own problems so that they could learn and grow. This fueled anger and resentment in my heart. I would say "yes" with my lips, but "no" with my heart. I was living a double life, and it was killing me.

Tragically, many people never become aware of the unresolved areas of their past that are keeping them stuck. Many are never unleashed into their full purpose and potential. Many are never freed up to serve and minister to others in healthy and productive ways because they are so weighed down by their own shame, unwanted behaviors, and sin. Many continue on, stuck in unwanted behaviors and subconscious ways of self-sabotaging.

Our unmet longings can communicate lies to us about ourselves, God, and the world around us. Over time, we can begin to adopt and live from the perspective of faulty core beliefs or wrong perceptions. We can begin to believe lies about ourselves deep down—"I'm unlovable," "Something is wrong with me," "I'm not good enough," or "I'm not loving enough." We can believe lies about others—"I can't trust anyone," "All authority figures are on a power trip and will use and abuse me," or "People who look different from me are uneducated and immoral." We can also believe lies about God—"He could never love or forgive me," "I can't depend on him," or "He's not good."

No matter how hard we may try to believe what is true, it can seem like there is something deep down that will never align with the truth. I (Ben) lived that way for decades. I didn't feel as though I fit in with my family—or my friends, for that matter. I thought that I could never meet the expectations of my parents and teachers.

Deep down, I started to believe the lie that I was inadequate and worthless. Although it was a lie, it felt like the truth. It dictated the way I lived and interacted with others. I was insecure, reactive, and angry, and I felt constantly overwhelmed and feared failure. Even when I began to recognize that this lie had taken deep root, it took years to see this change and to operate from a healthier place.

We'll dive deeper into this reality in the next chapter, but for now we want you to know that these unmet longings can shape how we begin to see everything in our lives, especially when these longings are rooted in childhood experiences. Childhood hurts may be painful to engage, but it is nonetheless important to do so because early experiences are often the most formative—we take those unresolved experiences with us into every stage of life. If we fail to engage our story—that is, to confront and understand the high and low places in our past—faulty core beliefs can arise repeatedly, and as longings go unmet we often react, cope, and try to escape in unhelpful ways.

You may be thinking, "I had a good life. I was never abused, never went through anything that painful, didn't experience anything traumatic, and had almost everything I needed." That may be true, but our memories can also play tricks on us; our experiences form the basis of what we think is normal. We all experience hurt, letdown, loss, and unmet longings in our past and present to some degree, even if we really did have the best friends, parents, siblings, and relatives. And, as we explored earlier, we can't reliably compare the impact of attacks and absences in our lives with those experienced by others. Unmet longings and unresolved hurts are unavoidable and universal.

We often struggle to figure out why we just can't seem to stop some of our unwanted behaviors. We can want so desperately to stop certain thoughts, beliefs, or actions, but we continue on in them. In this chapter, we will explore that missing link. This link will empower you to move beyond being stuck and into the thriving life God has for you. When we find out the missing link—our *why*—we find out our *how*. Specifically, how our unmet longings lead to unwanted behaviors and how we can overcome them and experience healing.

## More Than Our Nature

In the early chapters of this book, we introduced the foundational model we are exploring in this book, which we call "The Wholeness Apologetic." Next, we explored the first part of that model and explained how we experience wholeness and the abundant life God intends for all of us through the Seven Longings. In this chapter, we will explore the second part of the model—the fact that there is more driving our sin and our unwanted behaviors than just our fallen nature (see "Unmet Longings Lead to Unwanted Behaviors" in the Wholeness Apologetic diagram).

Here is the premise: We sin because we are born sinful, but we also sin and cope in reaction to being hurt and sinned against.

The first part of this premise is straightforward: we sin because we are born sinful. We agree with what Jesus and church leaders have taught for centuries, that we are born with a broken nature and, like every other human being, we have transgressed against a perfect and holy God (Romans 3:23). We live by our own rules. We love created things more than the Creator. We hurt ourselves and other people. Even the good we do is often done with mixed motives. We are born into this brokenness, experiencing the opposite of wholeness.

Despite all of these things, we are not worthless. We do bad things and we commit evil acts, but that doesn't change the fact that we are made in the image of God. We have inherent value and worth since we are the pinnacle of God's creation. Whether or not we have a personal relationship with Christ or call him our Lord, we still have infinite worth.

However, when we give our lives to Christ he adopts us into his royal family and calls us his own. He makes us righteous, blameless, and clean, forgiving us of all our sin—past, present, and future. He restores us to a similar state that the first humans experienced in Eden—having the full ability to choose to follow him, and to do good or bad. He comes to dwell inside us and empowers us to choose not to sin and to live in wholeness. His power gives us both the desire and the ability to pursue the fulfillment of our unmet longings in healthy and satisfying ways (Philippians 2:13). What amazing news! Imagine a world where people lived according to these beliefs. What a beautiful world filled with goodness that would be!

The second part of our premise, however, is less widely understood and acknowledged: we sin and cope in reaction to being hurt and sinned against. Let's explore this in part two of the Wholeness Apologetic model:

## THE WHOLENESS APOLOGETIC

Supporting God's design for human flourishing in all areas of life.
We experience this primarily through the fulfillment of our
Seven Longings with God, self, and others.

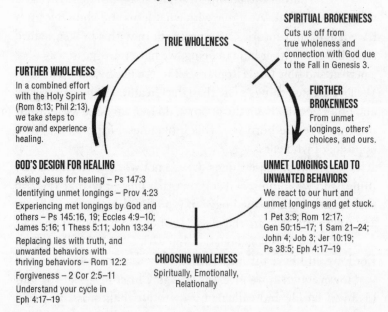

**SPIRITUAL BROKENNESS**
Cuts us off from
true wholeness and
connection with God due
to the Fall in Genesis 3.

**TRUE WHOLENESS**

**FURTHER WHOLENESS**
In a combined effort
with the Holy Spirit
(Rom 8:13; Phil 2:13),
we take steps to
grow and experience
healing.

**FURTHER BROKENNESS**
From unmet
longings, others'
choices, and ours.

**GOD'S DESIGN FOR HEALING**
Asking Jesus for healing – Ps 147:3
Identifying unmet longings – Prov 4:23
Experiencing met longings by God and
others – Ps 145:16, 19; Eccles 4:9–10;
James 5:16; 1 Thess 5:11; John 13:34
Replacing lies with truth, and
unwanted behaviors with
thriving behaviors – Rom 12:2
Forgiveness – 2 Cor 2:5–11
Understand your cycle in
Eph 4:17–19

**UNMET LONGINGS LEAD TO UNWANTED BEHAVIORS**
We react to our hurt and
unmet longings and get stuck.
1 Pet 3:9; Rom 12:17;
Gen 50:15–17; 1 Sam 21–24;
John 4; Job 3; Jer 10:19;
Ps 38:5; Eph 4:17–19

**CHOOSING WHOLENESS**
Spiritually, Emotionally,
Relationally

God makes it clear in Scripture: we not only sin due to the sinful nature we are born with (Psalm 51:1), but our tendency is to sin and react when we are hurt and sinned against. This is why Jesus told his followers, "Bless those who curse you, pray for those who abuse you" (Luke 6:28 ESV). It is why Paul wrote, "Repay no one evil for evil, but give thought to do what is honorable in the sight of all" (Romans 12:17 ESV), and Peter exhorted, "Do not repay evil with evil or insult with insult. On the contrary, repay evil with blessing, because to this you were called so that you may inherit a blessing" (1 Peter 3:9). Our natural reaction to being cursed, abused, and insulted is to lash out in sinful, retributive ways. We long for better things—to be treated fairly, respectfully, and kindly, for example—but when our legitimate longings for such treatment go unmet, our natural response is to take action. We repay evil with evil, hold a grudge, get angry and vengeful, start to hate ourselves, or cope with our hurt in ways that we hope will relieve the pain. Think about the last time you were criticized or insulted; your reaction was probably not to respond with compliments and blessings.

The life of Samson in the Bible can be read as a case study of our tendency to react sinfully when we are hurt and sinned against. His Philistine bride betrayed a confidence, so he lashed out and killed thirty men (Judges 14). He deserted his wife and then learned that she'd been given to another man, so he destroyed the Philistine fields and orchards, bringing retribution on his wife and her father (Judges 15). His own people, men of Judah, tried to turn him over to the Philistines to prevent a wider war, but Samson grabbed a donkey's jawbone and killed a thousand men at Ramath Lehi (Judges 15). And so it continued and escalated until a blinded, chained Samson destroyed himself and three thousand men and women in one final act of vengeance.

Throughout Scripture we see countless ways that individuals have sought to cope with their hurt, whether from being sinned against by someone or experiencing hurt from the world's brokenness. When David was on the run from King Saul who sought to kill him, David was riddled with anxiety and hiding in caves fearing for his life in 1 Samuel 21–24. Like David, how many metaphorical caves do we hide in to cope with our hurt, stress, and unmet longings? How many times do we become overwhelmed with fear in reaction to pain and stress in life?

We see Job, after losing his wife, kids, wealth, health, and crops, so depressed that he wished he had never been born (Job 3). We see Jonah responding in anger, wanting to withhold God's message of forgiveness from the Ninevites due to their history of brutality and violence against his people. We see the Samaritan woman so full of shame at being known for having five different husbands that she fetches water at the hottest point of the day when no one is around to avoid being seen (John 4).

Like these examples throughout Scripture, the hurt and unmet longings we experience in life can fester, leaving a lasting impact in our souls. We see this in Jeremiah 10:19 (ESV), "Woe is me because of my hurt! My wound is grievous. But I said, 'Truly this is an affliction, and I must bear it.'"

Like Samson's tragic storyline, our efforts to cope with our unmet longings and the ways we sin in response to hurts never lead to satisfaction. Our unwanted behaviors leave us in even more pain, as David said, "My wounds fester and are loathsome because of my sinful folly" (Psalm 38:5). Anger, unforgiveness, overeating, self-destructive thoughts and actions, and unwanted sexual thoughts and behaviors are often ways of dealing with the hurt and stress of unmet longings in our interactions with others.

This isn't to blame other people or circumstances for how we have responded to our hurt and unmet longings; we must "carry our own load" and own our choices. As Dr. Ted Roberts says, "That's not to say our addictive choices are caused by the actions of others. We made the choices. But if we don't understand the pain of our past, we can't reclaim the blessing and destiny God has set aside for us in the future."[3]

Dr. Mark Laaser expresses the similar purpose between our

ways of coping by sinning and the addictions people get caught up in. "Sin and addiction have some common characteristics. Like an addiction, sin is uncontrollable and unmanageable . . . Addictions provide a way of escape; a false solution; a means to control loneliness, anger, anxiety, and fear."[4] Whatever unwanted behaviors we are facing, they are all attempts to make life more manageable. All of our unwanted behaviors are ways of coping with our unmet longings and trying to relieve the hurt, fear, loneliness, or pain we feel.

While we know it is possible to face unmet longings and hurts from others and not respond in sin, as Jesus did, a sinful response is our tendency as humans. Jesus faced all kinds of pain, betrayal, and unmet longings and can empathize with us, but he didn't sin. Scripture makes this clear when it says Jesus was "tempted in every way, just as we are—yet he did not sin" (Hebrews 4:15). But as humans, we struggle with choosing to cope and sin versus choosing to live into wholeness.

I've heard many well-intended Christians say that we just need to "repent and believe" to overcome our unwanted behaviors. That we just need to confess our sin and ask Jesus to change us. That we must just read the Bible more, pray more, serve more, and love Jesus more and learn to hate our sin. All of those things are a good and necessary start, but if we stop there, if we don't invite Jesus's healing work into the deeper unresolved areas of our life, we halt short of the deeper freedom, healing, and intimacy that Jesus wants to bring.

I've heard many others say that until we hate our sin enough, we won't change. I understand where they are coming from, but people will struggle to fully hate their sin until they hate the sin done to them that has led to their unmet longings. Few of us are truly aware of the sin and injustice that has been done to us in this broken world. It's such a consistent part of life that we may brush it off as normal or be fearful of what we may uncover should we try to identify it—whether it's ways the Enemy has sought to destroy us, ways people have taken advantage of us, ways people close to us neglected or abandoned us, ways we have experienced racism or sexism, or more subtle ways we have been rejected and marginalized over and over. Being loved and treated justly doesn't inherently happen in this world, as Dr. John Perkins says: "justice is something for which every generation has to strive."[5] It's not about blaming others or playing the victim, but about facing reality, identifying our unmet longings, and grappling with our experiences so we can properly grieve and progressively step into healing.

We must first grieve and hate the sin and injustice done to us before we are truly able to grieve and hate the sin and injustice we do to God and others. Only then will we be able to understand the reality and painful effects our sin causes. Only then will we be able to understand, grieve, and heal from the unmet longings contributing to our unwanted behaviors.

## Listen to Your Longings

How do we begin to understand the connection between our unmet longings, our past hurts, and the unwanted behaviors we are stuck in? By listening to our longings, and by understanding the "why" of the type of unwanted behaviors we get caught in. The type of sin and unwanted behaviors we struggle with are determined by our hurts, life experiences, and unmet longings. Unwanted behaviors are ultimately not the problem; they merely point us to the problem.

God has given us an incredible gift to discern the source of our problems: our emotions. Drs. Dan Allender and Tremper Longman III share great insight into this:

> Ignoring our emotions is turning our back on reality; listening to our emotions ushers us into reality. And reality is where we meet God. . . . Emotions are the language of the soul. They are the cry that gives the heart a voice . . . In neglecting our intense emotions, we are false to ourselves and lose a wonderful opportunity to know God. We forget that change comes through brutal honesty and vulnerability before God.[6]

Emotions help us to get in touch with what is going on inside of us. You may not think of yourself as an emotional person, but you are; we all are. Emotions are part of what it means to be human. We are all designed to feel deeply and to be aware of what is going on inside of us. We are created to experience happiness, gratitude, excitement, sadness, anger, disgust, trust, and peace. In this we are like our Creator, who experiences emotions himself. Scripture depicts God expressing joy (Zephaniah 3:17), peace (John 14:27), grief (John 11:35), anger (Psalm 103:8), and many more emotions. Experiencing emotions is part of what it means to be made in God's image.

So what do emotions have to do with our unwanted behaviors? Well, emotions give us insight into what is going on inside of us, into what we are longing for. Whenever we experience emotions, we are experiencing either the fulfillment or unfulfillment of one or more of the Seven Longings we discussed earlier. So we must learn to listen to our longings. When you find yourself giving in to an unwanted behavior, ask yourself, "Which of the Seven Longings am I seeking out in this unwanted behavior?" Think about what happened the day of, the week before, and the month before. Think about what upcoming challenges you may be anticipating. What interactions with people caused your longings to go unmet? What circumstances in your life caused you to turn inward and start believing lies about yourself? What challenges have you faced that may have caused you to feel rejected, unsafe, or shameful? Was it being criticized by your boss, being left out by friends, or feeling overwhelmed with tasks to do? Was it feeling like a failure once again as you didn't measure up to your own expectations or someone else's? What longing might you have been fearing would go unmet in the future?

My friend Han would get overwhelmed and stressed out at work. He felt like he could never keep up with the workload. He often felt like a failure. Rather than talking about the emotions and lies he believed about himself, he'd isolate himself. He'd turn to video games and spend hours playing them. Once he started listening to his longings, Han realized that video games were a way for him to get the appreciation he craved. He felt like a failure at work, but in the video game world he was a hero accomplishing tasks and achieving goals. Every point he scored and every level he completed said to Han, "You're capable. You've done a great job." As he began challenging the lies he was believing about himself—that he was a failure, incompetent, and unappreciated—and reaching out to others for legitimate appreciation and encouragement, Han's use of video games as a coping mechanism began to decrease.

You'll be amazed at the understanding you'll gain as you listen to your longings. You'll find insights and answers as to why you continue returning to the same unwanted behaviors. As you get this initial practice down, begin taking it deeper. Ask yourself, "When was the first time this specific longing went unmet?" and "How has this longing gone unmet in past experiences?" These questions will help you understand the connection between the unmet longings of the past and how you've been seeking to fulfill them through unwanted behaviors for years. Only when we understand how brokenness has been at work in our lives can we understand the areas in which we need to experience wholeness.

In the past, I (Ben) experienced extreme anxiety prior to speaking engagements—so much so that I often contemplated backing out or hoped the engagement would get canceled. As I began seeking to understand the unmet longings driving my anxiety, I identified it as a fear of stumbling over my words, embarrassing myself, and not being accepted by the audience. The anxiety was not random; our unwanted behaviors never are. It was like a radar device, always on alert and trying to protect me from further rejection.

As I went further in listening to my longings, I explored the roots of that unmet longing. I remembered that in the second grade I began making short mumbling noises in school. The urge felt irresistible (much later, I found out that this was a symptom of a neurological disorder called Tourette's Syndrome). Once, I began to mumble quietly as my teacher was talking at the front of the classroom. She stopped suddenly, fixed an angry look on me, and snapped, "Ben, be quiet!" The whole class turned and stared at me. I froze. My heart raced. I felt terrified, humiliated, and ashamed. From that point on I feared group situations, at times even experiencing a dream-like state and feeling detached from my own body. I later learned that I was dissociating due to the hurt and embarrassment I had felt, and those painful experiences followed me into my adult life as a public speaker. My unmet longing for the assurance of safety and acceptance from my past hadn't gone away. It had led to unwanted behaviors of persistent anxiety and dissociation.

It's been said that all wounds heal with time, but that is simply not true. Only when I began listening to my longings, understanding how they had gone unmet in the past, and connecting the dots between my past and present did I begin to find freedom. By learning to quickly recognize my fear and the reason for it, I've begun to address the lies and unmet longings driving this fear with truth. I've begun to meditate on the acceptance and safety I experience in Christ, which has increased my freedom from fear.

As Han began listening to his longings and exploring his unmet need for appreciation, he recalled that as a child when he shared his opinions and feelings with his parents, he would often be told that he was wrong. Eventually he gave up, choosing not to share his feelings rather than being shut down when he did. He also experienced little encouragement when he performed well in school, so he figured, "No matter what I do, it's not going to be good enough." Those experiences and the hurts they caused carried through into his adult life. He began to see how he had been stuck in isolation and anger, resorting to compulsive video game playing as a way to seek the fulfillment of his longings, although the "fix" he sought was inadequate and ultimately unsatisfying.

Once we start listening to our longings, we can begin to

understand the cycle of brokenness at work in our lives. We can understand the subconscious ways we have continued down the same path over and over again. And we can finally begin to understand how to experience the lasting satisfaction that we are actually seeking out in our unwanted behaviors. This isn't ultimately about stopping the bad and starting the good, but about experiencing the fulfillment of our longings. This is about thriving. About flourishing. About wholeness. About living the life God created you to live!

## One Longing at a Time

As we start to understand our unmet longings and the hurts in our hearts, God invites us into healing and freedom as he meets those longings in healthy ways. He invites us to seek the fulfillment of our longings in something that will truly satisfy our hearts rather than cause our wounds to fester and remain unhealed by coping mechanisms, which ultimately lead to more pain and deeper infections of the soul. We'll get to the practical implications of this in future chapters. But, for now, begin the process of listening to your longings. Get in tune with what is going on inside of you. Take it one day at a time, one longing at a time.

After I (Josh) continued meeting weekly with Henry, I began to listen to my longings. Situation after situation came up where people asked me to come and speak or to help them with their problems in ministry. I began saying no. It was so hard. It cut against the grain of how I had learned to function and strive for acceptance for decades. But I had to do it. I realized I wasn't free, as Dr. Cloud taught me, until I could say no and walk away. This caused great fear and stress as I began to face my insecurities of what people would think or say to me when I said no. I felt disconnected from feeling accepted for some time as I learned how to get that longing fulfilled in healthy ways. It was like going through withdrawals. It was agonizing, but so worth it.

In the months that followed, I began to experience acceptance through meditating on Jesus Christ's acceptance and love for me. I began to engage more with my wife, Dottie, and experience her love for me and acceptance of me. I began to experience a sense of acceptance for who I was rather than what I could do. I began to experience healing, freedom, and the fulfillment of my longings in a much healthier and more satisfying way than ever before. These practices have continued to this day. I've learned that God often brings healing over time rather than in an instant; healing is usually a process, not a single event. He does this as he helps us unlearn certain thought processes and unhealthy ways of coping, and he empowers us by the Holy Spirit to walk in new ways. I'm still being healed from those deep wounds of my childhood, but God has brought me further than I ever could have dreamed.

Our unmet longings lead to unwanted behaviors. By understanding the unmet longings driving the unhealthy thoughts, patterns, and behaviors we want to change, we can begin to seek the fulfillment of these longings in healthy ways rather than destructive ones. By helping us understand the deeper issues behind our problems, Jesus can lead us to solutions to both.

## Questions for Reflection

1. Begin the practice of listening to your longings. Which of the Seven Longings might you be seeking out in your primary unwanted behaviors?
2. In what recent ways through interactions with people, circumstances, and events have those longings gone unmet?
3. What feelings and rewards do attempting to meet those unmet longings temporarily bring?
4. Why might this longing be of such significance for you? Where might this longing have gone unmet in your past?

# CHAPTER SIX

# WHAT YOUR BRAIN NEEDS YOU TO KNOW

I woke up wanting to die. It was a cold and overcast morning in February 2014, and I (Ben) woke to an overpowering weight beyond all sadness I had ever experienced before. I felt as if I was living in the depths of hell. I looked out the window, distressed, and thought, *Why am I feeling this way? How do I make it stop? God, what is going on?*

Gloom, exhaustion, worthlessness, hopelessness, and horror hit me like a tidal wave. Tears flowed, almost nonstop. The turmoil continued for days. I had experienced depression off and on throughout my life and had endured abuse, assault, addiction, and more, but never anything like this.

No one close to me had died. I hadn't lost my job. I hadn't experienced a relational heartbreak. There was no apparent reason for my emotional distress, but it was unbearable. Crippling. I lost my appetite. I didn't care to watch TV shows or movies that would normally have entertained me. I didn't want to spend time with friends. Happiness and hope fled; only sadness, terror, and evil remained. The only thing that seemed to bring me any respite was talking to God and experiencing his nearness. But the agony continued for days that felt like years. I feared that at some point I would end up attempting suicide.

It wasn't until a year later, as I went through an in-depth counseling process with Dr. Ted Roberts, that I began to understand what had led to that experience. This pattern of despair, although it had never been this pronounced before, had actually been developing for years at a subconscious level. It had started when I was a boy. As I shared earlier, my father was frequently angry with me, often lashing out when I'd misbehave or simply fail to meet his expectations. I seldom felt loved and accepted for who I was. In fact, I felt hated. Consequently, I developed a negative core belief that there was something wrong with me. I didn't just think I did wrong; I thought I *was* wrong. Inherently flawed and inadequate.

Sometimes I would fight back against my dad's anger and punishment, but that just seemed to make things worse. Often, I would just give up. I'd turn on myself and let the thoughts and beliefs of worthlessness run wild, further enforcing the lies being communicated to me. "I'm the problem." "Something is wrong with me . . . with who I am." "I'm not liked in this family." These thoughts became beliefs and my soul began to deeply hold them. Little did I know that those experiences would chart the course for much of my teenage years and young adult life.

This pattern of turning on myself and perpetuating lies of worthlessness, which began at an early age, had continued into adulthood. Whenever I messed up, didn't follow through, let someone down, didn't perform perfectly, or couldn't do what I had committed to, I would feel worthless. It was more of a feeling than a conscious thought. It was as if I was experiencing the emotions of all those painful times from the past at once—in the present. I felt as if I had no control, that my feelings were random, that there was some kind of misfortunate chemical imbalance in my brain leading me to feel deep sadness from time to time, which came to a debilitating culmination on that February morning in 2014.

## Blaming vs. Naming

There is a difference between blaming and naming. Blaming points the finger at someone; naming involves accepting, understanding, grieving, and forgiving. Naming involves identifying the underlying unresolved problems so we can heal and move toward a solution.

As I looked back on that February 2014 episode, I was able to name what had happened. In the weeks leading up to that morning, I had overcommitted to responsibilities in ministry: long days, hours upon hours of emotional investment, and countless meetings each week. I was doing too much. It was taxing. I was nearing exhaustion, but I didn't want to stop, despite not being able to do it all to the best of my abilities. I began to feel like a failure over and over. I didn't think I could abandon any of my responsibilities or commitments. I tried to push through, but eventually an overwhelming sense of inadequacy caught up with me.

Subconsciously, I had once again turned on myself. Negative thoughts about myself played on a never-ending loop in my heart and mind. The scripts from my past unmet longings and negative core beliefs about myself had overtaken me like an avalanche. Worse, I actually believed them on a deeply emotional level.

I've learned through the years that my experience wasn't unique. I've met countless men and women, young and old, around the world who are stuck in unhealthy thoughts and actions. More often than not, these patterns are taking place at a subconscious level. They are the default patterns people are living out of because they developed them early, even in childhood. Their spirit and core identity may have been transformed by Christ, but they haven't put off the old self (Ephesians 4:22) and put on the new self (Colossians 3:10). They have not fully experienced the newness of life that Christ offers (Romans 6:4). They haven't been transformed by the renewing of the mind (Romans 12:2). Many continue to live reactively, repeating old patterns, rather than proactively developing new patterns in Christ.

## The Battle of the Brain

God has a lot to say about the beautiful gift of our minds. The Bible mentions the words "mind," "think," "believe," and variations of those words over 580 times in the English Standard Version (ESV) alone. Throughout these mentions is a huge emphasis on where we are to put our mental energy. Colossians 3:2 tells us to set our minds on things above. Philippians 4:8 tells us to think about things that are true, noble, right, and pure. Romans 12:2 tells us to be transformed by the renewing of our minds.

Another important passage depicts our minds as battlefields:

> For though we live in the world, we do not wage war as the world does. The weapons we fight with are not the weapons of the world. On the contrary, they have divine power to demolish strongholds. We demolish arguments and every pretension that sets itself up against the knowledge of God, and we take captive every thought to make it obedient to Christ. And we will be ready to punish every act of disobedience, once your obedience is complete. (2 Corinthians 10:3–6)

The battles we must fight against unhealthy beliefs and unwanted behaviors are spiritual battles that take place primarily in our minds. Why is so much attention given throughout Scripture to what we are to do with our minds? Because our behavior follows our beliefs. The way we think influences what we do.

We see this in Ephesians 4:23–24, which tells us "to be made new in the attitude of your minds; and to put on the new self, created to be like God in true righteousness and holiness." Paul encourages us to first change the attitude of our minds, or the way we think, and to then take action—to put on the new self, to live into the ways of righteousness that are consistent with who we are in Christ. Our behaviors will follow what we truly believe.

Every day we see our behaviors following our beliefs. If you believe you're going to get a paycheck as a result of working hard at your job, you'll probably keep at it. As you continue working and consistently get a paycheck, the belief that you'll be paid for your work solidifies and your behavior will follow. If you believe the weather app on your phone is generally accurate (whether or not that belief is well founded), you will take an umbrella with you when rain is in the forecast. If you believe your office or school chair will support you when you sit, you will do so without checking it first.

We all have beliefs that influence what we do. Those beliefs become hardwired into our brains over time. Psychiatrist Norman Doidge, commenting on the work of psychiatrist Bruce Wexter, said:

> In childhood our brains readily shape themselves in response to the world, developing neuropsychological structures, which include our pictures or representations of the world. These structures form the neuronal basis for all our perceptual habits and beliefs, all the way up to complex ideologies. Like all plastic phenomena, these structures tend to get reinforced early on, if repeated, and become self-sustaining.[1]

In other words, every time we act on our beliefs, these beliefs are reinforced; over time and as a result of repetition, these beliefs get hardwired into our brains. I believe this is one of the reasons the Bible says, "Train up a child in the way he should go; even when he is old he will not depart from it" (Proverbs 22:6 ESV). Whether we are trained in healthy or unhealthy ways, intentionally or not, our experiences, especially as children, will form beliefs which in turn dictate behavior.

This all takes place in an area at the center of our brain, called the limbic system, which is the emotional center of our brains. Michael Dye, an expert in the field of addiction studies and counseling, describes the limbic system as "part of what the Bible calls your heart, the center of beliefs and emotions. . . . Thoughts and beliefs create emotions which drive behaviors."[2] In the limbic system our experiences in life get recorded, leading to our perceptions about ourselves and the world around us. Our painful experiences and our unmet longings etch neural pathways into our brains. These pathways are like well-worn hiking trails that our minds and emotions easily and repeatedly slip into, shaping how we live, think, and see life.

A core belief, simply put, is any deeply rooted perception you hold. Core beliefs can involve perceptions about nearly everything—spirituality, people, ourselves, culture, and hobbies. Many of our core beliefs tend to revolve around our perceptions about ourselves, God, and others. Those core beliefs can be contrary to what we *want* to believe. They can be illogical. For example, you may say, "I know that I am a gifted and valuable person, but deep down I often feel inadequate or worthless." Or, "I know that my spouse is trustworthy, but deep down I just know there's something going on." These core beliefs are developed over time through our experiences in life and are solidified as a result of our unmet longings.

We can also have positive core beliefs from experiencing our longings being met, especially in childhood as our brains are being developed. For example, children who had parents who accepted them as they were and encouraged and engaged them emotionally will more likely develop positive core beliefs about themselves and others—such as, "People are trustworthy and will usually come through," "People accept me for who I am," or "I have something of value to offer."

Those neural pathways in our limbic system, our emotional brain, will often overpower our rational thoughts because there are more pathways from the limbic system to the rational part of the brain than the other way around.[3] So, when we have repeated experiences with unmet longings and deeply rooted lies stemming from those experiences, those beliefs will often overpower the truths we want to believe, no matter how hard we try. No matter how hard we may fight to believe what is true, it can seem like something deep down in us will never agree. Those unmet longings can shape how we begin to see everything in our lives, especially when we experienced those unmet longings in childhood.

Some of us find it painful to reflect on our childhood experiences; we would rather just forget. But your unwanted behaviors are indications that you haven't forgotten—or at least your limbic system hasn't. It's important to look at childhood experiences (among others) because they are some of the most formative that we take with us into every stage of life. If we fail to engage with our past experiences, those negative core beliefs will come up again and again. We take the chance that suppressing negative things in our past will simply reinforce the negative results of those experiences in our present and future.

## Behavior Follows Belief

As we go throughout our lives, the lies we believe are triggered by our circumstances. Your boyfriend or girlfriend breaks up with you. Your boss criticizes you. An overwhelming task is handed to you. A friend disagrees with you. The kids refuse to listen to you. Your longings go unmet—again—and those unmet longings trigger your negative core beliefs. They feel so real and true in the moment. When this happens, you want to escape the stress and pain as quickly as possible; you want to feel better. You attempt to have your longings met in an unhealthy way.

A few years ago, I (Ben) was mentoring a college student, and as we started to talk about his life growing up, he shared how he often didn't feel accepted for who he was. He felt like he couldn't measure up to his parents' expectations. His grades were never up to their standards. His parents said he was too emotional. He struggled to fit in with his friends. He had a deep longing to be accepted for who he was—a need that often went unmet. As we talked week after week about the recent times he became angry or the times he went to porn, sure enough, there was always an incident right before these instances that left him feeling rejected or inadequate. He had been caught in this cycle for years. His anger and porn use were ways for him to feel in control, attempt to protect himself, and receive a hit of dopamine.

The following diagram is an attempt to visually explain this cycle, representing how circumstances in our present-day life can trigger our unmet longings and negative core beliefs, leading us back to our unwanted behaviors.

## UNWANTED BEHAVIOR CYCLE

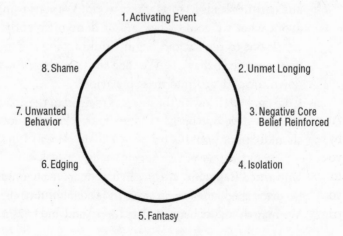

1. Activating Event
2. Unmet Longing
3. Negative Core Belief Reinforced
4. Isolation
5. Fantasy
6. Edging
7. Unwanted Behavior
8. Shame

1. **Activating Event.** A situation or circumstance that produces in you—consciously or subconsciously—an awareness of your need. Someone hurts you, you were anticipating a reward or pleasure that didn't happen, or you didn't perform a task as well as you had hoped. There are countless activating events in our daily lives, all of which are unique to our personal stories.

2. **Unmet Longing.** When we experience an activating event, we feel the pain of one or more of our Seven Longings going unmet. We may not recognize the unmet need, but we experience the pain.

3. **Negative Core Belief Reinforced.** When we experience an unmet longing, it triggers or reinforces the negative core beliefs and lies we believe, carving the pathway in the brain a little deeper and affirming the lies that have already taken root.

4. **Isolation.** Next, our tendency is to separate, even isolate, ourselves from other people and situations that (in our minds, at least) may maintain or increase our pain. Rather than dealing with what is going on inside of us, we ignore it or try to outrun it.

5. **Fantasy.** Trying to escape the unmet longing, situations, and core lies leads us to a fantasy world. We start thinking about what we could have said or done differently. We check out of reality and begin thinking about going to our unwanted behaviors. We then start plotting how to go down the path again to these behaviors.

6. **Edging.** We flirt with the idea of giving in to the cravings. "I'll just have one beer." "I'll just take a look." "I know I shouldn't, but just this once." We edge closer to the line we swore we'd never cross again.

7. **Unwanted Behavior.** We give in once more to an unwanted behavior, slipping into a rut we've traveled many times before. We may think we just ended up there suddenly because we

weren't strong enough or the temptation surprised us, but in reality we took a predictable—and preventable—path to get there.

8. **Shame.** The cycle leads inevitably to shame. Our unmet longings were never truly satisfied. The core lies are further reinforced. The unwanted behaviors are repeated, and we are as vulnerable as before to repeating the entire cycle the next time an activating event occurs.

Sometimes we go through this eight-step process in a matter of seconds. For example, if someone criticizes you, your longing for acceptance goes unmet and it feeds the core lie that you're inadequate. You get angry and isolate yourself from that person. You fantasize about how you should have responded, edge closer to your typical unwanted behavior, and then give in to it. Afterward, you feel ashamed and beat yourself up for your weakness and bad choices.

At other times, the process unfolds more slowly. But each time we go through this Unwanted Behavior Cycle, it sends us spiraling downward. Over time, our choices cause a physiological change in our brains. As we make decisions, our brain neurons or nerve cells are firing away, transmitting chemical signals to one another.[4]

Neuroscientist Carla Shatz says, "Neurons that fire together wire together."[5] We create fixed brain pathways of thinking and responding to life, similar to the muscle memory we develop when learning how to play an instrument or ride a bike. Over time, this begins to feel natural, even instinctive, making it progressively easier to repeat the same compulsive or unwanted behaviors we wish we could change.

Have you ever driven home from work or school, started daydreaming, and arrive home without remembering thinking in depth about all the turns you took to get there? Have you ever found yourself gravitating to the same seat or section at church, a work meeting, or school? Have you ever found yourself picking up your phone and checking your notifications without consciously thinking about it? Have you ever found yourself thinking about what you're going to do over the weekend as you work out at the gym, and yet your body keeps exercising even though your mind is elsewhere? These are all examples of your brain utilizing fixed neurological pathways that have already been developed.

One of the reasons we repeatedly resort to certain behaviors is that our brain rewards us with a chemical called dopamine. Dopamine brings about feelings of happiness and pleasure.[6] Our brains release dopamine when we do healthy things like having a life-giving conversation with a friend, listening to our favorite songs, and eating tasty food. But our brains also release dopamine when we indulge in unhealthy behaviors such as overeating, overspending, excessive gaming, and wasting time on social media. This release of dopamine conditions us to associate those activities with feeling good, making the process of overcoming unwanted behaviors as difficult as learning to walk on your hands instead of on your feet. That's why, as badly as we want to stop unwanted behaviors, we can be stuck in these cycles for years. Our unwanted behaviors are not just a sin issue, a hurt issue, or an unhealthy pattern issue. Our unwanted behaviors quickly become a brain issue.

Whether you realize it or not, you've developed fixed ways of thinking and acting for all your life. You have deeply embedded ways of making sense of the world around you. God wired you this way so that you could function efficiently and effectively at the numerous choices you make on a daily basis. Consider your morning routine, for example. You wake, open your eyes, move your arm, turn off the alarm, throw back the bedcovers, sit up, stand, walk to the bathroom, turn on the light, walk to the sink, pick up the toothbrush, open the toothpaste and squeeze it onto the toothbrush, turn on the faucet, wet the toothbrush, lift the brush to your mouth, open your mouth, and so on—just to brush your teeth! But you don't think about those individual and disparate decisions and actions. You've done each one many times before, so your brain and body perform as if on autopilot without consciously thinking through those decisions—or the thousands (millions, even) of decisions you make throughout the day.

Most of those decisions have been hardwired into your brain to free you to think and make other decisions. As Dr. Ted Roberts says, "It has been estimated that 90 percent of the decisions you make on a daily basis are unconscious in nature."[7] Those "autopilot decisions" are beautiful and amazing when they involve healthy (or neutral) things, such as walking, eating, looking both ways when we cross the street, etc. But when our unmet longings and negative core beliefs lead to the development of such autopilot responses, they turn into habitual, unwanted behaviors that need to be addressed.

## Hope for Your Brain

In spite of the negative core beliefs that have been embedded in our souls and the unwanted behaviors that have rewired our brains, there is great news. Just as God created our bodies to fight infections, he designed our brains for healing as well. The Bible affirms God's power—and the part we can play—to transform our brains: "Do not conform to the pattern of this world, but be transformed by the renewing of your mind" (Romans 12:2).

Several decades ago, neuroscience made an astounding discovery in identifying something called "neuroplasticity"—the capacity of the human brain to change its own structure and function through thought and activity.[8] In other words, modern science underscores what the Apostle Paul wrote two thousand years ago. While our identity in Christ never changes, our minds can be renewed and reprogrammed. Our negative core beliefs and unwanted behaviors can be overcome by the power of the Holy Spirit as we develop new core beliefs based on biblical truth.

When we take steps to renew our minds, God uses every little thought and action to transform our lives by his power, which science affirms. Doidge writes,

Neuroplastic research has shown us that every sustained activity ever mapped—including physical activities, sensory activities, learning, thinking, and imagining—changes the brain as well as the mind. Cultural ideas and activities are no exception. Our brains are modified by the cultural activities we do—be they reading, studying music, or learning new languages. We all have what might be called a culturally modified brain, and as cultures evolve, they continually lead to new changes in the brain.[9]

Just as neurons in our brains wire together over time, they also unwire. Doidge says, "Neurons that fire apart wire apart."[10] Our brains can change. We can develop new positive core beliefs and overcome our unwanted behaviors.

As we fight mental battles, challenge negative core beliefs, and have new experiences based on the truth of who God is and how he sees us, we can develop new positive core beliefs. Neuroscientist Dr. Caroline Leaf says, "As we think, we change the physical nature of our brain. As we consciously direct our thinking, we can wire out toxic patterns of thinking and replace them with healthy thoughts."[11] This is what it means to be transformed by the renewing of our minds. As we focus on the truth of who Christ is and who we are, and learn to experience and counter the lies with those truths, confronting and challenging them with God's Word, we can renew our minds and overcome our unwanted behaviors.

I (Ben) began to experience healing and freedom as I recognized the Unwanted Behavior Cycle in my life. I realized that activating events—like being excluded from social gatherings, feeling rejected by others, having overwhelming tasks to complete, or seeing an ex-girlfriend—all led to different unmet longings. My unmet longings then triggered my past negative core beliefs of worthlessness, inadequacy, distrust of others, and fear of abandonment, which would then lead me into a downward spiral that prompted unwanted behaviors and, eventually, shame.

As I started to catch myself at the activating event, invite Jesus in, call a friend for support, challenge the lies, and affirm the truth, I stopped going down the same destructive pathways. I developed healthy biblical patterns of responding to life's challenges. Over time, this developed new brain pathways and I began to thrive and experience the fulfillment of my longings in healthy ways. The old unhealthy paths in my brain became less traveled, so to speak, making it easier to choose healthy patterns. I stopped returning to unwanted behaviors like porn, overeating, overwhelming sadness, and deep anger as Jesus brought transformation by the renewing of my mind. This doesn't mean I no longer have unwanted behaviors or negative core beliefs, but they have less power, enticement, and grip on my life as Jesus continues to heal me by the renewing of my mind. To this day, it has been years since I have fallen into pornography or indulged in compulsive overeating. I still have activating events and suffer temptation in other ways, like anyone, but I can feel the effects of my new neurological pathways and changed desires, and I'm living in victory through the Holy Spirit's power.

This battle of the brain, being transformed by the renewing of our minds, is a cooperative effort between our choices and God's power. We don't just "let go and let God." It is the result of our partnership with God, the fulfillment of Romans 8:13: "For if you live according to the flesh you will die, but if by the Spirit you put to death the deeds of the body, you will live" (ESV).

In this battle, we must challenge the lies we have come to believe whenever they come up. We take those lies and unhealthy thoughts captive, and counter them with the truth of who Christ is and who he sees us to be. We live into what is actually true and experience it. We identify how those negative core beliefs were developed in our lives, and we identify all the ways they come up throughout our circumstances. We tell ourselves the truth so we can rewire the paths the lies created. We ask the Holy Spirit to mature us, help us believe the truth, and give us new experiences of having our longings met rather than seeing them go unmet and perpetuating the lies. We develop positive core beliefs. We fight the spiritual battle taking place in our minds and the deception that the Father of Lies (see John 8:44) wants us to believe. We understand the past, the lies, and how they come up today, and we begin living into wholeness rather than brokenness. Living into wholeness means understanding and living into the truth that combats the lies—truth about who God is, who we are, and how we are to live in relation to others. We invite you to continue in your journey to wholeness as you lean into truth in relationships, expose the lies, and take steps toward wholeness (and a key way to begin and continue that process is by joining us in the *Resolution Movement* we've mentioned in this book).[12] In the next few chapters we will dive into practical ways we can renew our minds, providing hope through proven principles and practices that can overcome our unwanted behaviors and lead us into the thriving life we crave.

## Questions for Reflection

1. What negative core beliefs about yourself might you have developed from your unmet longings?
2. What negative core beliefs about God might you have developed from your unmet longings?
3. What negative core beliefs about others might you have developed from your unmet longings?
4. What are 2 or 3 common activating events in your life that lead to unmet longings and reinforce some of these negative core beliefs?

# YOU'VE GOT THE WRONG GOD

In late July 2018, I (Ben) received an unexpected text from my friend Teddy regarding our mutual friend, Alex: "He doesn't have much time to live. The best thing you could do is to come and see him." Alex had been fighting an aggressive form of brain cancer since his early twenties. The next day, I was on a plane flying across the country to Virginia to see Alex.

Alex was one of my best friends in college and remained a close friend. He had been through rounds of chemo and radiation and had gone into remission a few years before. But the cancer had come back. His body wasn't responding well to the treatment, leaving him with internal bleeding and brain swelling, so he had to cease chemo.

When I arrived in Virginia and saw Alex, his energy was drained and he could hardly sit up, but we were able to have a short conversation. Over the next few days, the vibrant, animated, and passionate man I had known for years slipped away. He was losing the ability to keep his eyes open, along with the ability to talk and eat. He was increasingly incoherent. He was deteriorating by the day. I sat with him for hours. Some days I sat in silence, with my hand on his shoulder. He couldn't talk or open his eyes, but he could hear me and feel my presence. Each day overflowed with grief as the reality set in.

Within a week of the text from Teddy, Alex passed into eternity at the age of 29, leaving behind his wife of two years and their almost-four-month-old son. It made no sense to me. It seemed unreal. Of all people, of all life situations, of all ages to die. Why? How? I was in shock. In the weeks to come, past conversations, old jokes, and key moments we had shared together came to mind. Songs we used to listen to came on in my car, and I would move to text Alex before remembering the new reality. My eyes frequently flooded with tears.

Over the following months, a subtle anger at God grew inside me as I experienced further loss and pain: struggles with direction in ministry, the sudden death of a coworker, the end of a dating relationship. Eventually, my anger began to inhibit my functioning. I had trouble thinking clearly and enjoying the normal simplicities of life. I wrestled with God. I was honest with him. I shared my feelings with others, so as not to bear the burden alone. In my dialogue with God, he reminded me of how I had learned to overcome my anger in the past, that throughout my life anger had been a way of dealing with fear—of rejection, not being safe, and being hurt. How fear and anger are two sides of the same coin. How, much of the time, anger is a way to protect ourselves when we're afraid. Anger had been my way of trying to regain control and keep others at a distance. I began to ask what the fear was behind my anger toward God, and soon realized that I was afraid God wasn't who I thought. I feared that he wasn't safe, he didn't have good in store for me, and he was going to hurt me like others had. As I addressed those lies, remembered God's past faithfulness and goodness to me, and asked him to forgive me for my anger toward him, the anger began to dissipate.

A few days later, I was sharing my anger and fears with Dr. Ted Roberts. He smiled and chuckled, "If that's what God's like, we're all hosed! There's no hope for anyone." I burst into laughter. He was so right.

This reminder from Dr. Ted and the doubt I had experienced about God's character which was manifested through my emotions and anger took me back to several years earlier when I'd struggled more deeply with who I believed God to be. It was several months into my initial stages of healing, and I was meeting with Dr. Ted weekly. I had come to my appointment prepared to share about the fears in my life and what I thought the future would hold. I began to share how I thought God had nothing but suffering and pain in store for my life. I feared the future greatly. I believed my worst years were ahead of me.

Dr. Ted said, "You've got the wrong God!"

This shocked me. I'd had a personal relationship with Christ for two decades. I spent regular time in prayer and reading God's Word. I'd taken seminary classes. I studied theology in my spare time. How could I have the wrong God?

Over the course of the coming months, I realized that deep within my soul I viewed God as angry and obsessed with rules. Intellectually I knew God loved me, and had done much good in my life, but on a deep emotional level I believed lies about God that were overflowing into the way I viewed myself, lived my life, and treated other people. I had bought into a false narrative about who God is and how he relates to us.

Throughout this book and in the *Resolution Movement* we've launched, we've talked about our God-given Seven Longings, the ways in which we're wired for relationships, and how we can be hurt in ways that affect our core beliefs and perceptions about the world around us. The way to experiencing the deepest fulfillment of our longings, overcoming unwanted behaviors, and thriving in life is to understand and experience God for who he truly is as an engaged loving Father who wants to satisfy our deepest longings in healthy ways. While we need others to meet our longings, God is the primary source; he often meets our longings through other people, but he also does so through our personal relationship with him. When others fail, he doesn't. When longings go unmet in relationships, we can always trust him to meet our longings. He will always accept us, show his love to us, be available to us, and so on, through our personal relationship with him. We need others to meet our longings, especially as children, but we are created to have a healthy balance between God meeting our longings directly and through the agency of others around us. We were created to experience spiritual wholeness, the completeness that comes from knowing and experiencing God for who he truly is. This chapter, and Chapters 8 and 9, form the basis of how we can begin to live into wholeness in greater depths with God, ourselves, and others (see "Choosing Wholeness" in the Wholeness Apologetic diagram).

## Do You Have the Wrong God?

Maybe, like me, you've had negative core beliefs about who God is. Maybe you know (intellectually, at least) that God is loving, forgiving, and always there for you, but deep down you struggle to believe this. Maybe intellectually you believe that Jesus truly meant it when he said "it is finished," and that he once and for all purchased salvation, a new identity, and forgiveness for you, but you find yourself hustling for your worth and seeking the approval of others.

Maybe, deep down, you think that God is always angry with you, walking around with a cosmic two-by-four waiting for you to mess up so he can punish you. Maybe you think that God hates fun—that he is a prude, a cosmic killjoy who gave humanity a bunch of pointless and impossible-to-follow rules. Maybe you see God as someone who created the world and then stepped away—someone who is disengaged from his creation and generally unconcerned with your pain and suffering.

As we've traveled the world meeting people and ministering

to them, we've found that many have the wrong God—they don't see him for who he truly is. They harbor wrong assumptions and core beliefs about his character. They see him as (or suspect him to be) angry, obsessed with rules, and distant.

These views about God are toxic to our wellbeing and prevent us from thriving in life. Fulfillment in life comes from knowing our Creator, experiencing his love for us, and understanding his intention for us to flourish. Such negative core beliefs about God spring from two primary sources: wrong teaching and painful experiences.

When wrong perceptions about God's character have been taught and modeled to us, they can become deeply embedded lies. Ultimately, we view God through the lens of either truth or untruth. Many of us view God through lenses shaped by our own shame and the negative core beliefs we've formed about ourselves. As the authors of the book *The Cure* say, "Your view of you is the greatest commentary on your view of God."[1] We can't help but see God through the lens of our own brokenness.

Additionally, many churches, preachers, teachers, and influencers communicate wrong things about God. Some elevate certain divine characteristics over others. They may teach about the holiness of God while neglecting to teach that God is also gracious and forgiving. Some may teach that God is disappointed in us and angry whenever we mess up rather than teaching that he loves us despite what we do. Others may teach that God lets everything slide, and that he has no standards and no characteristics besides love. Some have taught that God is intensely angry and only now loves and tolerates us as a result of Christ's work on the cross, as opposed to his love being the reason Jesus chose the cross.

Maybe you have had experiences of growing up in a church, community, or family that over-emphasized rules and put little emphasis on relationships. Maybe you had experiences with a teacher, parent, or spiritual leader who was angry, absent, or obsessed with rules and had the highest of expectations. Maybe whenever you didn't perform as expected or couldn't meet others' standards you were judged, shamed, or punished. Maybe you've come to believe that God is that way too.

## We All Have "Daddy Issues"

God is referred to as our Father throughout Scripture, so often a person's view of God is filtered through the lens of an earthly father. In some cases that's good, of course, but in others it presents an obstacle to an accurate, biblical perception of God.

My friend, Norm Wakefield, once shared with me the impact his experiences with his father had on his view of God:

It wasn't until I reached middle adulthood that I was able to establish a warm, friendly relationship with my father. My dad's career was filled with pressures and discouragements. He had difficulty enjoying his children, and we found it difficult to approach him.

I remember placing my faith in Jesus Christ at age twelve— the first member of my family to become a Christian. But as I began to form a mental image of my heavenly Father's love for me, I couldn't help superimposing my relationship with my earthly father. Since my dad never seemed to be satisfied with me, I felt God must feel the same way. It was as if he were saying, "Norm, why don't you straighten up? Why do I have to put up with you? You'd better get your act together, young man, or I'm going to . . ."

You can imagine the impact these ideas had on my self-image as a young teen, let alone my misperception of the love of God! It is very common for children to think God values them in the same way their own fathers regard them. If Dad is loving, warm, and nurturing, they tend to picture God as loving, warm, and nurturing. But if Dad is perceived as cold, distant, and occupied with "more important things," they are likely to feel that God is unapproachable and uninterested in them as individuals.[2]

Today, it's not uncommon for fathers and mothers to be even further disengaged due to technology. Don't get me wrong, I love technology and it is an incredible gift from God, but I constantly see parents out with their kids, and their solution for bad behavior or their kids' restlessness is to hand them a phone or tablet to watch a show or play a video game rather than engaging their little hearts. Parents are more distracted and disengaged than ever, due to all the technology fighting for their attention. Streaming services, social media, calls, texts, and notifications so easily distract and prevent us from engaging with our kids. Parents can easily fall into the trap of modeling being "alone together" rather than meeting their kids' longings and helping them develop the necessary social skills to engage others and experience relational satisfaction.

When a parent (particularly a father) has been absent, hurtful, disengaged, or inattentive to our Seven Longings, we can't help but feel those unmet longings. We develop what many call a "father wound" or "daddy issues." These experiences with our earthly fathers will often translate into how we view other fathers in general, including our heavenly Father. I once heard William Paul Young say, "It took me all of fifty years to wipe the face of my father completely off the face of God."[3] Some of us, like him, may see an angry, disapproving face every time we think about God. And how we learn to navigate all our relationships in life is drawn from our primary and foundational relationships with key figures like our fathers. For better or worse, our first relationships in life are likely to chart the course we will follow in other relationships, including our relationship with God.

As I (Ben) experienced rejection and anger from my father, I began to see God the same way. I began to obsess about my salvation. I thought God would reject me too when I stood before him after death. I thought my occasional doubts about his existence meant that I wasn't really saved and didn't really have a personal relationship with him. I began to wish I had never been born because I thought it would be less painful than to die and spend eternity in hell. For nearly ten years, I prayed the "sinner's prayer" up to twenty times a day in an attempt to finally, maybe, have the assurance of being with God for eternity. I lived in agony and mental torture. How I wish I had seen my heavenly Father all those years for who he is.

Of course, no one has a perfect father. We've all been let down or hurt at some point by our fathers. I don't say this to blame anyone nor to minimize anyone's pain, but simply to understand where our wrong perceptions of God have come from so we can move forward into wholeness.

If you're questioning whether or not you have wrong perceptions about God, here are some common examples of what these beliefs and actions can look like. These may not be conscious thoughts, but are negative core beliefs deep within our hearts and minds that bear fruit in our actions:

- I do good things to try to earn the love and acceptance of God.
- I often worry about the future, my safety, and finances, doubting God's provision.
- I feel like God is distant from me when I sin and is waiting for me to get my life together.
- I think God is often disappointed in me.
- I believe God loves me but doesn't really like me. He just tolerates me.
- I think God loves me more when I perform, do good, or fulfill religious duties.
- I think God is obsessed with rules and regulations.
- I believe God is consistently angry with me due to my choices.

- I think God isn't going to be there when I need him the most.
- I think God couldn't possibly forgive me or love me after what I've done.

God created us and designed how we are to live and thrive in this world. If we have a distorted view of God, our beliefs and behaviors will be distorted as well. If we have a low view of the Creator, we can't help but have a low view of the created. We will struggle with our worth, purpose, and direction in life. We may also view others as angry, distant, or not safe. We will struggle to grow, experience happiness, and live life to the full.

## A God Who Knows What It's like

Maybe, as a result of the suffering, tragedy, or abuse you have experienced, you've concluded that God doesn't exist. Surely, if he did, he wouldn't have let such things happen to you. Or maybe you believe there is a God but that he isn't good; otherwise, he would have prevented these things from happening. I have had similar thoughts, questions, and assumptions. There are no easy answers to the thoughts and questions prompted by deep and lingering pain. But God knows what it is like to suffer, to be betrayed by his closest friends, to be publicly humiliated, abandoned, abused, beaten and whipped beyond recognition, and executed for crimes he did not commit.

God is not ignorant of or indifferent to the pain and hardships that come with being human. He walked among us in the person of Jesus Christ. He faced greater suffering, trauma, and unmet longings than anyone in world history. He sympathizes with us. While Jesus was fully God when he walked this earth, he was also fully human, wired with Seven Longings like the rest of us. He felt deeply. He continues to feel deeply.

He weeps when we weep. He knows what pain is. He knows

how bad it can be. He can handle our doubts, questions, and fears. And one day he will put an end to all hurt, evil, pain, and suffering. Justice will be served, and wrongs will be made right.

It's also important to note that good and evil cannot exist unless God exists. If there isn't a creator and we are all the result of a random and purposeless accident, then the concepts of good and evil are social constructs without any objective basis. However, God did not create evil and suffering; they are the absence or lack of the goodness of God. As darkness is defined by the absence of light, evil is defined by its relation to good; it is "parasitic on something good," as Augustine of Hippo once said.[4] Evil and suffering come, not from God but from hearts, lives, places, and things that ignore or oppose God.

## What If God Isn't Who You Think?

Many different opinions exist about who God is and isn't. Pantheists say that God is everything, and everything is God; they see him as a cosmic life force that includes all substances of the universe. Polytheists believe in multiple gods and goddesses, who either control different aspects of creation like the weather or protect some individuals and harm others. Deists believe in a supreme being who created everything that exists but is uninvolved in any further way with creation, like a master clockmaker who designed the world, wound it up, and has since let it run on its own, without his care or intervention.

Christians, however, believe in one God who is a personal being who existed before time and space as we know it. He spoke the words "Let there be . . . ," and by the power of his will all that exists came into being (Genesis 1:3). We believe these words came from the voice of a personal, infinite God who "created everything there is—nothing exists that he didn't make" (John 1:3 TLB).

The questions naturally arise: what is the nature of this God, is he knowable, and why did he create us? While a God with the power to create vast universes is bound to be beyond our comprehension in many ways, he is knowable to us finite creatures. But how? Although we cannot know him exhaustively, we can know him truly, sufficiently, and with confidence because of what he has revealed about himself to us.

For example, he is eternal, without beginning or end (Isaiah 40:28). He is omnipotent, almighty and powerful (Job 42:2). He is omnipresent, everywhere at once (Jeremiah 23:23–24). He is immutable, never changing (Psalm 102:26–27). He is omniscient, all-knowing (Isaiah 46:9–10). He is triune, a unity and a trinity of Father, Son, and Holy Spirit (Genesis 1:26; Matthew 28:19; Luke 3:22; John 15:26). The Father loved us enough to send his Son (1 John 4:14). His Son loved us enough to sacrifice himself (John 10:18). The Holy Spirit loved us enough to enter our lives and make our relationship with God real, personal, and intimate (John 14:26). He is a loving Father (1 John 4:8), engaging and personal (Psalm 46:1; Philippians 4:19), gracious (Psalm 145:8) and forgiving (1 John 1:9).

While it is difficult for some to believe, God loves each of us (John 3:16; 1 John 4:8–10). John Eldredge writes:

> You are the son of a kind, strong, and engaged Father, a Father wise enough to guide you in the Way, generous enough to provide for your journey, offering to walk with you every step.
>
> This is perhaps *the* hardest thing for us to believe—really believe, down deep in our hearts, so that it changes us forever, changes the way we approach each day.[5]

Because of the unmet longings in our past we struggle to see God as he is, and therefore struggle to see ourselves as we truly are, as God sees us. As a result, we are susceptible to lies based on our pain instead of living and thriving according to the truth.

Another reason it can be hard to understand that God loves us is that many of us view love as simply a feeling. Love can result in a feeling, but it isn't a feeling. Love is an act of the will to protect and provide. We know this for several reasons. One, we see countless examples of God's love as an action—Christ dying on the cross for us (Romans 5:8), the Father providing us with his only son Jesus (John 3:16), and Christ giving himself up for us (Galatians 2:20). Second, you cannot command a feeling, but you can command an action, and we are commanded to love: "Dear friends, let us love one another, for love comes from God. Everyone who loves has been born of God and knows God. Whoever does not love does not know God, because God is love" (1 John 4:7–8). Third, emotions come and go, but love is an everlasting commitment, or covenant. God said to Israel, "I have loved you with an everlasting love" in Jeremiah 31:3. He always keeps his "covenant of love" with his children and keeps on loving to a thousand generations (Deuteronomy 7:9). God's delight in us, his obsession with us as his children, and his passion for relationship with us are all acts of his will. God has so much more than feelings toward us. He has promises, commitments, and an unstoppable and fierce act of his will to protect and provide—real love.

God is a loving Father who demonstrates his love to us by protecting us and providing for us. If you've had a challenging relationship with your father or other authority figures in your life, this can be hard to grasp. But it's true, nonetheless, and it's not a feeling that comes and goes; it is his nature and his will to love you.

## God Loved You before You Took Your First Breath

I talk to many people, young and old, who don't realize that God loved them even before they became Christians. While we were in darkness, when we were still enemies of God, he loved us and died for us (Ephesians 5:8, Romans 5:8). He loved us first (1 John 4:19). He did not wait for us to clean up our act. He did not wait for us to meet his expectations. He did not wait for us to make him proud. He simply loved us. Not only that, but he showed his love for us.

He is not the kind of father who has trouble hugging a child or saying, "I love you." He is not the kind of father who has "more important things to do." He loves us foremost (Romans 8:32). He spoke his love for us with the Word (John 1:14). He showed his love to us on a cross. He wrote his love for us in blood.

The Father not only loves us first and foremost, but he also loves us forever (Jeremiah 31:3). The Father's love for us is complete, constant, and unconditional. We cannot earn it. We cannot escape it. We cannot erase it. He may be disappointed in our actions when we disobey him, or saddened when we stray from him, or sorrowful when we sin, but he never, never, never stops loving us. These things grieve his heart because they disconnect us from closeness to him, not because he is uptight about our behavior. Our Father's unconditional love for us is such that "neither death nor life, neither angels nor demons, neither the present nor the future, nor any powers, neither height nor depth, nor anything else in all creation, will be able to separate us from the love of God that is in Christ Jesus our Lord" (Romans 8:38–39).

As author Sally Lloyd-Jones puts it, God loves us with a "Never Stopping, Never Giving Up, Unbreaking, Always and Forever Love."[6]

God is also personal, kind, and engaging. He needs nothing, yet still desires to have an intimate, personal relationship with you and me. He created humans because he wanted us to have a love relationship with him. It is through this relationship that we find wholeness that results in true joy and happiness.

He is a personal God who invites us to come as we are, not as we should be, because we will never be as we should be in this life. He accepts us in spite of our weakness. He enters our world. He identifies with us. He is engaged in the finite details of our lives. He cares deeply for us. He knows our thoughts. He invites us to cast all of our cares upon him (1 Peter 5:7). He cares about what we care about. He is a greater Father than we could ever fathom.

Have you ever known or witnessed a father like this? One who is personal and cares deeply for his kids? My friend Daniel is one of the most loving and engaging fathers I know. He cherishes his little boys. He jokes with them, plays with them, and seeks to meet their desires.

Recently, a couple of Daniel's sons began to love dinosaurs, as many kids do. So he bought an inflatable T-Rex costume. One day after school, Daniel threw on the costume and awaited the arrival of his boys on the school bus. When the bus pulled up in front of the house, out came Daniel, the Jurassic Dad, running through the front lawn. The boys were thrilled as their dad began to chase them. Laughs, smiles, and excitement filled their hearts. As cool as it was that their dad had transformed into a T-Rex in front of all their friends, what was cooler is they knew the love and engagement of their father. They knew that their dad loved them relentlessly, took interest in what they liked, and went out of his way to engage their hearts.

Do you know who your heavenly Father truly is? Can you grasp how much he loves you and all the ways he is seeking to engage you personally throughout each day? The subtle surprises and the good gifts you receive every day that you may not always recognize as the affections of your Father? He lavishes love on us day in and day out, though we are often unaware of it. Those times you find a new delicious type of food or drink, the times you are able to fall asleep and wake up rested, the songs you hear that breathe life into your soul, and the happiness you experience from simple pleasures—these are all ways God shows who he is and how much he loves you.

Billy Graham once said, "God proved his love on the Cross. When Christ hung, and bled, and died, it was God saying to the world, 'I love you.'"[7] What God did for millions, he did for one, *you*. Were you the only human to ever exist, he would have come to earth, died on the cross, and risen from the grave taking your sin to restore a relationship with you. His love for you is reckless, relentless, passionate, and pursuing. He isn't obsessed with your sin or your shortcomings; he's obsessed with you.

## You Can See God as He Truly Is

No matter what we have experienced, believed, or been taught about the character of God, he desires to restore our view of him. He wants us to experience him as our true, loving, heavenly Father who is personal and engaging, as happened for my friend, Norm, whom I quoted earlier in this chapter:

> I had this mistaken image of God until my forties, when he brought some circumstances my way that literally transformed my relationship with him. I discovered what a loving, caring, vitally interested God he is! And interestingly enough, it was through these same circumstances that the walls finally came down, and my father and I were able to draw much closer together than we had ever been.
>
> As part of my fresh discovery of the nature of God, I read through the Psalms with pen in hand, noting every mention of the Lord. As I studied these verses, I realized that almost every reference provided either a direct or indirect description of our heavenly Father. I soon had several notebook pages filled with these attributes, and from them emerged a profile of what most of us would consider an "ideal" father. My conclusion? The basic qualities of fatherhood that are seen in our Lord are the qualities he desires to form in today's Christian fathers.
>
> I had discovered a theology of fatherhood—with God himself as the role model![8]

Although I (Josh) had been fortunate to find great models of fatherhood through a couple men in my life, Norm helped me see that I had neglected the greatest model of all—the original, the standard of effective fatherhood—God himself. The mental picture I had of the kind of father I wanted to be was actually a picture of my heavenly Father, who is the source of all good things (James 1:17).

He is "the Father, from whom all things came" (1 Corinthians 8:6). He breathed the breath of life into the first man, and Adam became the first "son of God" (Luke 3:38). From that moment, each of us have been made in the likeness of our Father and Creator, who made us and formed us (Deuteronomy 32:6). Literally, from day one God has not only desired a Father-child relationship with each one of us, but he has also modeled what a healthy fatherhood looks like.

God is a tender Father who invites us to address him as "Abba," the Aramaic equivalent of "Daddy" or "Dada" (Romans 8:15; Galatians 4:6). He is a listening Father who bids us to approach him boldly as "our Father in heaven" (Matthew 6:9). He is a loving Father who freely and forcefully demonstrated his Father-love at the baptism of his Son, Jesus, with a voice like thunder that said, "This is my Son, whom I love; with him I am well pleased" (Matthew 3:17). He is a giving Father who gives good gifts to his children (Matthew 7:11). He is the Father of all (Ephesians 4:6), the very definition of fatherhood, the fount of everything that is good, moral, and worthy of imitation.

The characteristics I had longed for and missed in my own father were characteristics of God. This understanding, this realization, matured and empowered me. I no longer had to feel crippled by my earthly father's example. I no longer had to struggle to form a clear picture of what a father should be or of the father I should be. My needs and longings could be met in God, the Model Father!

We have a greater Father who can heal our "father wounds." We have a greater "daddy" who can overcome our "daddy issues." We have a God who promises to meet all of our needs and longings. Do you see God as he truly is? Do you experience his fatherly love and nearness? He desires to meet your desires. He desires to know you at a deep personal level and to bring about satisfaction and wholeness through a close relationship with him.

If you have yet to enter into a personal relationship with God, you can begin right now. The Bible says that we are born sinful and in a state of alienation from God.[9] But God desires to forgive us of our wrongs and our sin and restore us to a relationship with him.[10] This is why God sent Jesus to live the perfect life of obedience to God[11] that we were incapable of living, die on the cross taking the penalty for our sins,[12] and rise from the dead, conquering sin[13] and offering us forgiveness and a restored relationship with God.[14] Through Jesus alone[15] and not by any good deeds or behavior,[16] we can have forgiveness and a reconciled relationship with God simply by asking him.[17] This is grace, unmerited favor freely given to us by God! If you don't have a personal relationship with God, we invite you to begin that relationship today. Simply pray (talk to God) and say, "God, I want a personal relationship with you. I desire to surrender all of my life to you. Please forgive me, through Jesus alone, of my sin and all the wrongs I've ever done, all the ways I've turned against you, myself, and others. Come into my life and take control from this moment on."

If you have just entered into a personal relationship with God, we welcome you into the family of God, eternal life, and the thriving life you were designed to live! This is the best and most important decision you can ever make. For the next steps in your new relationship with God, check out the Additional Resources section in the back of this book.

Wherever you are in your journey, I invite you to consider implementing some of the following steps that God has used to help us continue to grow in seeing and experiencing God for who he truly is, being transformed by the renewing of our minds.

- Regularly remembering what God has done in your life
- Talking to him throughout the day
- Daily thanking him for five good things he did or gave you that day
- Reading the Bible through the lens of who God truly is as a loving and engaging Father

- Looking for the good gifts, the subtle things, that are his love and kindness to you
- Reading books by authors who see God as he truly is
- Listening to teachers and preachers who teach from the Scriptures and have an emphasis on who we are as his beloved, cherished, righteous sons and daughters
- Meditating daily on who God is as your loving Father
- Hanging out with people who model God's love and engagement to you
- Getting to know and observing loving fathers who are engaging with their kids
- Being quick to take wrong thoughts about God captive and remind yourself who he actually is
- Identifying and working through the negative experiences, wrong messages, and unmet longings you have from past experiences with your father, authority figures, and/or spiritual teachers
- Identifying the practical ways God has and is (directly and through other people in your life) currently meeting your Seven Longings

## Questions for Reflection

1. What negative core beliefs might you have about God?
2. What unmet longings, painful experiences, or past relationships with authority figures might have contributed to these beliefs?
3. What one positive core belief about who God truly is do you want to develop?
4. What fathers in your life model well who God truly is, so that you can intentionally learn from them?

# SEEING YOURSELF AS GOD SEES YOU

**D**o you have a photo of your spouse, significant other, or children as your phone background, eager to show them off at the first opportunity to anyone and everyone? What about your driver's license photo? Do you delightedly show it to others? Pass it around at parties? Copy it to your online profile? Or do you cringe every time you see it, as I do? Do you pray for the day when you'll renew your license in the hope that the photo will be at least a little better? Why is that? Is it because the Department of Motor Vehicles seems skilled at taking the worst possible photos? Okay, maybe it's that. But it may also be that your driver's license photo doesn't represent what you really look like.

Each of us carries another personal identification photo, one that is far more important than any photograph in our phone, wallet, or purse. It is a mental self-portrait, our concept of who we are. Like your driver's license photo, your inner self-portrait may or may not accurately represent the real you. Just as the quality of a photograph is diminished by lack of focus, poor lighting, or faulty camera settings, your inner self-portrait may be inaccurate due to faulty or incomplete input and distorted programming you've received about who you are.

Take Alex, for example. The prevailing message he heard growing up was, "Alex, you can't do anything right." Was it an accurate portrayal of him? No! He may have been inept in some areas, as we all are. But to say he couldn't do *anything* right was a demeaning and grossly inaccurate assessment. Yet that message was imprinted on the film of Alex's heart from childhood. Today he carries that distorted self-portrait wherever he goes— the picture of a thirty-two-year-old man who sees himself as little more than a mistake, a failure just waiting to happen. He's embarrassed to reveal his presumed identity to others, so he is shy and anti-social.

On the other hand, consider Theresa, whose perception of herself is suitable for framing. She grew up in a home where she was cherished and nurtured by loving, Christian parents. She learned early that she was God's unique and dearly loved creation. As a result, she entered adulthood confident of her worth to God and to others. She meets new people easily, and God has used her to bring a number of her new friends to Christ.

How do you feel about your inner self-portrait? Is it like Alex's, a picture that embarrasses you, one you would rather keep hidden? Or is it more like Theresa's, a representation of your true identity as a child of God? I speak to tens of thousands of adults and young people every year, and I visit with hundreds of them personally after the meetings. Sadly, few have the positive, nurturing background that Theresa enjoyed. More often, they nurture inner self-portraits that are badly out of focus—struggling in life because of their difficult home life, the culture around them, or unbiblical experiences (or some combination of the three) that have obscured their true identity.

All of the unmet longings we've experienced can lead to negative core beliefs about ourselves. Throughout life, especially in our early years, we look to people's actions and words to determine our significance and value. Over time we buy into what people say or communicate to us about our worth, which can lead to a distorted view of ourselves. Maybe for you it was being bullied or rejected by others. Maybe others approved of you when you performed well but didn't approve of you when you failed. Maybe you weren't allowed to express your opinions, or you felt largely ignored. Any of these scenarios, intentional or not, can convey a lack of value, leading us to develop negative core beliefs about our worth and leading to shame—believing "I am bad" or "something is wrong with who I am." As much as we may "know," intellectually, that we are loved and valued for who we are, we struggle to "own" that reality. Even though we may receive compliments or kudos from others, these seem to roll off our backs rather than meeting our needs.

Author and researcher Brené Brown says, "Shame is the most powerful, master emotion. It's the fear that we're not good enough."[1] The lie of shame can be deeply embedded within our souls, often disguising itself as humility, keeping us trapped from being who God made us to be.

I'm convinced that shame is at the core of most of our personal struggles in life, second only to (and cooperating with) the sinful nature we are born with. We react and get angry out of insecurity. We blame others or our circumstances rather than owning our mistakes. We find unhealthy ways to cope with our stress and pain because we don't believe we can do better or be better. So many of us are fighting the wrong battles. We wage war on our unwanted behaviors, which only causes us to think about them all the more. Of course, we need to seek the help of God and others for our unwanted behaviors, and we need to have a plan and receive support as we put the plan into action. But instead of being hyper-focused on a particular behavior, we need to understand our unmet longings and negative core beliefs that contribute to those unwanted behaviors. We need to take those thoughts captive and make them obedient to the truth of Christ. We need to believe the truth of who we are and live according to our true identity. The more we do this, the more our behavior will align with the truth, unwanted behaviors will lose their appeal, and we will experience the emotional wholeness we were created for: the completeness that comes from knowing and experiencing our God-given value and identity. As our unmet longings trigger our negative core beliefs, our primary battle lies many steps before our moments of temptation. The battle begins with developing new, positive, and accurate core beliefs about self, God, and others and then trusting God to provide new experiences that help us solidify these beliefs.

## A Case of Mistaken Identity

Sadly, the bright dawn of the third millennium has found so many people—Christians included—stressed out, unhappy, unfulfilled, and even despondent. Why? Because so many are unsure about their true identity. Even the church sometimes clouds the identity issue by overstressing the old sinful nature, which for believers was crucified and buried with Christ.

Our sense of identity can be negatively affected when we hear ourselves referred to as "converted sinners." After all, we don't call a butterfly a "converted caterpillar." It's a butterfly now; the old is gone, the new has come. When we trust Christ, we become new creatures. Old things pass away, and all things become new (see 2 Corinthians 5:17).

My hunch is that many fear what would happen if people stopped seeing themselves as "converted sinners" and regarded themselves as "saints" (Ephesians 5:3 ESV). Would they become prideful and arrogant? Would they disregard God's commands because they know they're loved and forgiven and God delights in them no matter what? Would they sin all the more because their shame would no longer inhibit them? I don't think so. I think, instead, they'd have a more intimate personal relationship with

God, make a greater impact in the world, and desire to obey God because they have experienced how much he loves them and cares for them.

It's no wonder our world struggles so much with shame and negative core beliefs about self. Shame and a false sense of self are nothing new. Our world is in a crisis of mistaken identity and has been since the first humans walked this earth. Shame has been the number one tactic of the Enemy since the creation of humanity. And, as we've said in previous chapters, Satan is the Father of Lies, so let us not be unaware of his most effective tactics against us.

As we discussed earlier, when Adam and Eve turned against God in the Garden of Eden, they immediately realized they were naked and became ashamed. They sewed fig leaves together to cover themselves. Then, as they heard the sound of God walking in the garden, they hid from him in their fear. It was a tragic scene. Perfect harmony with God had been destroyed. It was the first time Adam and Eve had ever been ashamed and afraid, and the first time they had hidden from God. Having known only wholeness, they experienced the effects of brokenness. It was all a result of believing lies about God, themselves, and each other.

Shame, which God did not want for us to experience, had entered the world, and has since passed down from generation to generation, plaguing humanity. But notice that instead of accusing Adam and Eve and adding to their shame, God approached them with curiosity and kindness. He knew the fear, the hurt, and the tragedy of what had happened and what they were feeling. His primary focus was not on their sin; he focused on his relationship with them because he loved them deeply. His heart was broken. Lies believed. Trust broken. Disconnection. Intimacy lost. But instead of berating them or shaking a finger at them, he said, "Where are you?" (Genesis 3:9). In Hebrew, "where" can be translated several different ways: "How," "What," "Where?" I imagine his fatherly heart, shattered, not seeking information but sparking illumination: "What are you doing?" "Why are you hiding?" "You know how much I love and care for you. You know who I am. You know you don't have to be afraid."

God didn't ask because he didn't know. He is all-knowing. He asked because he is personal and wanted to show his fatherly and compassionate heart to his children, to engage their hearts, and to reconnect with them after the disconnection that had just taken place. How often do we first call out people's sin rather than engage them with curiosity and kindness? How often do we heap more shame on them, leading to disconnection and lost intimacy? How often do we first say, "You're sinful and separated from God, but he wants to forgive you," rather than first engaging people with God's love and kindness, saying, "What have you been through? What hurts and unmet longings have you endured? God is radically in love with you and wants to know you personally, heal you, and invite you into the life you were created for." After all, it's God's kindness that leads us to repentance (see Romans 2:4).

And we see Adam's response, not leaping out from behind the shrubbery, saying, "Here I am," but explaining what had happened. He said he had heard God, was naked, became afraid, and so hid (Genesis 3:10). He was ashamed of himself and his actions, and not only did his behavior result from believing lies, but it also led him to believe more lies about himself and God. God asked, "Who told you . . . ?" (Genesis 3:11). God knew the heart of his beloved children. He knew they had believed a lie, and that they had fallen for the serpent's slander. And so it is with us. How many people have "told us" a lie about God, ourselves, or others—whether through words, actions, or experiences? This is the primary tactic of the Enemy when it comes to our unmet longings—using people, situations, and experiences to get us to buy into shame and negative core beliefs.

Adam responded and simultaneously blamed Eve and God, saying, "The woman you put here with me—she gave me some fruit from the tree, and I ate it" (Genesis 3:12). Wow. Not the smartest move for Adam. He felt shame, so he tried to blame others! Shamed people blame other people. They want to get the negative beliefs and feelings off of themselves as quickly as possible. They don't want to feel like they are the only people "in the wrong." But while Adam pointed the finger, God opened his arms. He responded with kindness and grace.

Next, God asked Eve; she, also full of shame, passed the blame to the serpent, explaining that he had deceived her (Genesis 3:13). Then followed the first consequence. God first addressed the one who victimized them—the serpent, Satan—before giving Adam and Eve consequences for their choices. God cursed the serpent and promised that one day the serpent would no longer have any power (Genesis 3:14–15). One day, he'd no longer be able to manipulate, victimize, or tempt God's children. One day, he'd be conquered by the magnificent plan that God had laid out to redeem humanity through the life, death, and resurrection of Jesus to rid the world of the consequences that this tragedy brought. Yes, Adam and Eve knew what they were doing in their disobedience, but they were also manipulated by evil. God is a God of justice. He first went after the victimizer, the deceiver—Satan, the Father of Lies.

Then God turned to Adam and Eve, but instead of cursing them as he did the serpent, he announced the consequences their choices had brought into the world (Genesis 3:16–19): Pain, suffering, physical and spiritual death, separation from God, and a power struggle between man and woman.

All of this prompts the question, "Who told *you*?" Who told *you* the lies that shamed you and contributed to the negative core beliefs you have about yourself? Who told you that you were worthless, unlovable, or just a face in the crowd? What unmet longings in the past and present have led you to this conclusion about yourself? Was it a parent? A sibling? A friend or significant other? Was it a teacher or spiritual leader? Whatever the case may be, you've suffered the consequences of those lies long enough. You don't have to cling to them any longer. You can choose to hear God say, "Who told you?" and replace the lies of others—even yourself—with the truth of God.

## Worthless?

People with a clear view of their true identity feel significant. They understand that they matter to God and to others, and that the world is a better place because they are here. They are able to interact with others and appreciate their worth without feeling threatened. They radiate hope, joy, and trust because they are secure in their identity as God's children. They accept themselves as lovable, worthy, and competent members of God's creation, redeemed and reconciled to God to become all he wants them to be.

However, those with a cloudy view of their identity as God's creation display a number of debilitating traits. The most common ways a clouded identity manifests itself is through the negative core beliefs of being worthless, unlovable, or just a face in the crowd.

Sebastian grew up in a Latino family in South America before moving to the United States as a child. Early on, his dad would physically abuse him, his siblings, and his mom. His dad was angry, aggressive, and violent. As an adult, Sebastian had a haunting sense that something was wrong with him deep down. He had a negative self-image, a faulty self-portrait. He felt inadequate. He procrastinated, struggled in school, and got stuck in many unwanted behaviors as he tried to make his life seem more manageable. A sense of shame and worthlessness showed in the way he carried himself—hunched shoulders, timid, quiet, distracted, and emotionally elsewhere. He came across as passive, a pushover, and unsure of himself and his life purpose. Even as a Christian, he struggled to feel any sense of self-worth. He loved God with all of his heart, but he struggled to truly see himself through God's eyes.

Like Sebastian you may believe that you are worthless, that

God simply tolerates you, or that he loves you but doesn't really like you. Maybe you wouldn't put it just that way, but ask yourself if you identify with any of the statements in the following list.

- ☐ I don't know or truly believe what God says about my true value
- ☐ I find myself hustling and striving for a sense of worth
- ☐ I obsess about my physical appearance, personality, and what people think
- ☐ I often fear rejection
- ☐ I worry about people abandoning me
- ☐ I am embarrassed easily
- ☐ I often feel inadequate, incapable, or not good enough
- ☐ I feel sad about myself at times
- ☐ I find myself trying to prove my value through success, name dropping, approval of others, or material possessions
- ☐ I struggle with procrastination
- ☐ I greatly fear failure
- ☐ I neglect my emotional and physical needs

Maybe you'd say that "worthless" is too strong of a word for what you feel, but you believe that you aren't good enough—you feel inadequate, insecure, insignificant. Welcome to the club. Ever since shame entered the world, doubts about our worth have plagued all of us. We get caught in the shame hustle—fighting to get some sense of value from status, relationships, material possessions, and achievements. Trying to perform to get our worth from anyone—whether it's ourselves, God, or other people—will always end in futility. Performance is the essence of manmade religion, which teaches you to do good in an attempt to be loved by God. But Christianity teaches that since we are already loved by God, we do good as a result. We don't do good in order to earn God's love; the good we do is the product of having received God's love, along with the result of his Spirit living within us.

Think: if we could get identity from our performance, then Jesus died in vain. Jesus's mission on earth was to live the kind of perfect life we could never live, fully obeying the Father, and to die, taking the punishment and separation from God that we deserved as a result of our rebellion and sin. Jesus took the blame for our sins, took our shame upon himself, and paid the price to achieve the approval of God for us. It's done. Through Jesus, we can be fully loved and fully approved of by God.

## Unlovable?

I (Ben) still vividly recall one time when I was sitting in the back of my parents' van. My friend and I were in fifth grade, and we were on the way to the pool in our swimsuits with our shirts off. He looked at me and said, "I'm fat, but not as fat as you." His words shocked me. I felt hurt, confusion, and sadness all at once. Before that moment, I was blind to physical self-image. But in a moment, my belief about myself changed; something I had never thought of before became all-consuming. I felt what Adam and Eve might have felt when they suddenly realized they were naked and became ashamed, seeing what they didn't see before.

That comment from my friend became the basis of my physical identity for years. As I was bullied in high school for being slightly overweight, that sense of being unattractive and unlovable compounded. I tried to escape that reality. Minimal eating, skipping meals, crash dieting, over-exercising, losing significant weight out of willpower then bingeing on food when I got sick of not seeing the hoped-for results. I wanted to escape those feelings of failure. I longed to be lovable.

This unmet longing led me to overeat compulsively, eventually gaining over 100 pounds. For several years, I ate whatever I wanted, whenever I wanted it. I used food as a way to avoid the pain of my unmet longings. I loved the temporary escape junk food brought me. I hid my behavior. I would go to fast food places, buy tons of food, then trash the "evidence" to avoid feeling shamed for overeating. I'd engage in this unwanted behavior alone, for fear of someone judging me. But I was ashamed, nonetheless. I was afraid, so I hid. Although overeating brought me some pleasure, it just sent me into a further downward spiral of shame and negative core beliefs about myself. Fat, unattractive, undisciplined, out-of-control. Unlovable.

You may not have struggled with overeating, but you may have had unmet longings and experiences that have led you to believe you were unlovable. Consider how this negative core belief may be manifested in your life by asking yourself if you identify with any of the statements in the following list.

- ☐ I fear what other people will say or do in response to my thoughts or actions
- ☐ I struggle with people-pleasing or doing whatever it takes to "keep the peace" with others
- ☐ I think if people really knew me—or what I've done— they'd reject me
- ☐ I struggle with anger
- ☐ I get very sad or angry when I feel left out
- ☐ I'm afraid of being fully known
- ☐ I struggle to open up about how I'm really feeling
- ☐ I can be overly sensitive and get hurt easily
- ☐ I feel like I'm a burden to people and a drain on their time
- ☐ I don't like who I am and struggle to love myself
- ☐ I don't like or love aspects of myself—physical traits, personality traits, etc.

## Just a Face in the Crowd?

Aliyah grew up in a Middle Eastern family in the United States. From an early age, she didn't feel personally valued. She thought of herself as one piece of a greater community which was valued over the individual. The decisions she made in her personal life were often the topic of conversation with her parents, making them either happy or disappointed over how the family was represented. Many interactions seemed to be about the family's reputation rather than about her as an individual. She felt like just a face in the crowd.

Aliyah told me,

> Even when I thought about God's love, it didn't feel specific. I thought of myself as a part of the package deal, sort of like God sent out a mass text saying he loved us and I somehow managed to get myself included on that text. Reading scripture like Psalm 139 didn't resonate with me the way it did with my friends who grew up in a world that shaped them to know that individuals are valued over community. I'm continuing to ask God to rewire my heart to understand that I'm his masterpiece, created by Christ Jesus to do good works. Not an afterthought, but an intentional creation by God with a specific plan and purpose.

Like Aliyah, many of us can feel like we're just a number, a face in the crowd. Just one of seven-billion-some humans walking this earth, not much different than the next individual. We can hear things like "God created us" or "Jesus died on the cross for our sins and wants a personal relationship with us" and yet not receive them as personal and specific to us. We may think God created us, sure, but more or less like products of a factory assembly line rather than being involved in the fine details of uniquely wiring and gifting us. We may wonder about our significance and if it really matters whether or not we're here. Consider how this negative core belief may be manifest in your life by asking yourself if you identify with any of the statements in the following list.

☐ I believe that Jesus died for all, but wouldn't have died just for me

☐ I struggle with my purpose and direction in life

☐ I seldom think much about myself and my needs

☐ I struggle with motivation

☐ I don't see how the world is a better place because I'm here

☐ I don't think people care that I'm alive

☐ I don't see my unique contribution to this world

☐ I don't think I'm unique, gifted, and here to make an impact on the world

Whether we struggle with a sense of being worthless, unlovable, or just a face in the crowd, many of us harbor negative core beliefs about ourselves. Like Adam and Eve we feel shame and fear, so we hide. We indulge in unwanted behaviors. We isolate from God and others. We run, never slowing down for fear of what we may discover. And our metaphorical fig leaves are ultimately as ineffective as theirs were (Genesis 3:7).

## All New Fig Leaves

People still use fig leaves. These days, however, they're figurative fig leaves. They're still an attempt to cover our shame, and they come in different styles: false confidence, overworking, sarcasm, standoffishness, and other unwanted behaviors. These gratify, but they never satisfy. They aren't just problems; they are pseudo-solutions. They are temporary and ineffective, no matter how often we hide behind them.

We have a better option—a real solution, one that is full of freedom. One that leads to thriving and wholeness. A cure for our shame, fear, and hiding. A cure that has already been achieved for us: the fulfilled promise that God made in the Garden of Eden when he cursed the serpent. This cure comes from the personal relationship and identity we can freely receive through Jesus as sons and daughters of God. Employing the metaphor of a mask instead of the fig leaves, the authors of *The Cure* write, "If this life of Christ in us is true—if there is no condemnation, if he's perfectly working to mature us from the inside out and if he's absolutely crazy about us despite all our stuff—why would any of us ever put on a mask again?"[2] Unless we allow others to see our true selves, only our false self will receive love. When we are afraid, hide, and carry shame, what we fear the most is what we need the most—being fully known and fully loved. Experiencing our true self being loved by God and others is the antidote to shame and our negative core beliefs about ourselves.

It's easy to get caught in the shame hustle, straining and striving to feel a sense of love and worth through our actions and people's approval of us rather than just being our true selves. But we are "human beings," not "human doings." It's easy for us, as Christians, to hide behind spiritual disciplines and ways of serving others to feel good about ourselves: A mission trip overseas. Tireless hours serving. Daily Bible reading. Rigid church attendance. Countless prayer meetings. We can feel good about ourselves and think we're closer to God based on our religious performance. All of these are good things, but when we do them out of negative core beliefs about ourselves, we can get lost in the activities as an attempt to "pay God back" for his work on the cross or as a way to "get closer to God." However, these can just be ways of putting ourselves under the law rather than operating in the freedom of God's grace. We can't get closer to God than we already are in Christ.

As Josh tells us in his book *See Yourself as God Sees You*,

Whether we like it or not, our perception of who we are has a great influence on our emotional, relational, and spiritual well-being. Research has shown that we tend to act in harmony with what we perceive ourselves to be. For example, children who are ridiculed as incompetent grow up tending to make more mistakes. People who believe themselves to be unattractive often have difficulty maintaining healthy friendships. If you see yourself as a failure, you will find some way to fail no matter how hard you want to succeed. If you see yourself as adequate and capable because of your relationship with God, you will face life with greater optimism and perform nearer to your best.[3]

Many people arrive at adulthood with a skewed sense of their worth to God and others. As a result, they have a skewed sense of their true identity. Our parents and teachers, the media, the marketing and advertising world, and even some of our religious experiences have reinforced the notion that our identity is shaped by the way we look, how we perform, and what we achieve. Even when we understand the truth, it is difficult to break away from the ingrained thought patterns that influence our behavior in these areas.

We are similar to the circus elephant whose leg is attached to a stake with a bicycle chain. How can such a flimsy chain restrain such a powerful animal? The creature remains chained because of a memory. The chain was first attached when it was very young, and every effort to pull free proved futile. The elephant learned that the chain was stronger than it was, and it carried this lesson into adulthood. Though strong enough as a full-grown elephant to escape, he is conditioned to captivity.

Our perception of identity works similarly. From childhood we are so conditioned to the importance of appearance, performance, and status that we remain bound to false notions even when we know better. But the truth about who you are is stronger than the flimsy chains that have kept you from realizing your full potential as God's unique, valued creation. You can experience freedom from those internalized bonds. You can participate fully in the joy, meaning, and fulfillment that are your inheritance as a child of God.

## Your True Identity

Whether you are regarded as somebody or nobody in your family, job, school, or church, you are somebody to God. Whether you achieve great or small things, your infinite worth and value to him are undiminished. God thinks highly of you and wants you to see yourself as he sees you. He wants you to live a life of spiritual, emotional, and relational wholeness—a thriving life.

Some may say, "But that's not biblical; the Bible says not to think highly of yourself." That's not quite accurate. Romans 12:3 says, "Do not think of yourself more highly than you ought, but rather think of yourself with sober judgment." God's Word does not tell us to have a low view of ourselves, but to have an *accurate* view of ourselves. How should we think of ourselves? A healthy self-image is seeing yourself as God sees you—no more and no less. That is God's standard. That is a healthy self-image and identity. The question is, "How does God see me?"

God says that you are of infinite worth; you are loved and unique. This isn't wishful thinking. This isn't "self-help." This isn't about pulling yourself up by your bootstraps or thinking happy thoughts. It's about truth, obedience to God, and a right understanding of his Word. It is a right understanding of what he says about you, and about living the life you were meant to live.

We can't just drum up some subjective standard of our worth as the basis of our value and life. We need something outside of ourselves, as humans, to define our worth. There has to be an objective and universal standard of value from an outside source greater than ourselves. If you paid for a one-pound bag of flour, only to get it home and find that it contained only ¼ pound, you might be confused, even angry. Say you take it back to the store and confront the store manager, who says, "That's our standard. We call that a one-pound bag. What you call it is up to you." That would be ridiculous, of course, because justice and commerce depend on reliable, objective, universal standards (there's even an International Bureau of Weights and Measurements that defines such standards).

Many of us use a similarly ridiculous measurement of our own value and worth. We accept a person's criticism or compliment as our standard. We measure our value based on our success or failure, our looks, or our status. But there is a universal and unchanging standard we can look to for our worth.

## You Are of Great Value

You are valuable. Anyone who communicated to you that you are worthless or unimportant was mistaken. It is essential that you see yourself as valuable, because that is how God sees you.

Society says that our worth is based on our accomplishments, success, looks, status, retirement plan, and life insurance policy. Even *Time* magazine valued the average human life at $129,000.[4] That's absurd. There is a universal and objective standard that determines our value, just as there is a standard for weights and measurements. This universal standard comes from the Creator, the manufacturer, the all-powerful God of the universe. We know this inherently as humans. This is why we abhor slavery, murder, rape, and human trafficking.

You are valuable because you are made in the image of God (see Genesis 1:27), meaning that you possess distinct dignity, value, a rational mind, moral desires, and relational capacity. The entire earth was entrusted to you to rule and reign over (see Genesis 1:28). God created humans with his own hands and breathed into them the breath of life, unlike animals or other created things (see Genesis 2:7). He created humans as the pinnacle of his creation and said they are "very good" (see Genesis 1:31). No one in the history of the world has the same personality, characteristics, or physical attributes that you have. You are an original. God chose to create you exactly how you are with your unique gifts, personality, and physical features.

Though sin entered the world through Adam and Eve, and you were born with a sinful nature (Psalm 51:5), you were still created in the image of God (Genesis 9:6). Nothing you do or have done will ever diminish God's love for you or your intrinsic value.

One of King David's psalms details beautifully just how much we are worth to God.

> What are mere mortals that you should think
>> about them,
>>> human beings that you should care for them?
> Yet you made them only a little lower than God
>> and crowned them with glory and honor.
> You gave them charge of everything you made,
>> putting all things under their authority.
>>> (Psalm 8:4–6 NLT)

You are also infinitely valuable, irreplaceable, and indispensable (1 Corinthians 12:22) because God gave his only Son to reconcile you to himself, paying an incalculable ransom that says that you are infinitely valuable. Your value wasn't created by Jesus's death on the cross; it was shown by Jesus's death on the cross. At Calvary, God declared to heaven, hell, and the whole earth that you are worth the gift of Jesus Christ, his dearly loved Son. If you ever put a price tag on yourself, it would have to read "Jesus," because that is what God paid to save you (see 1 Corinthians 6:19–20; 1 Peter 1:18–19). Your value isn't derived from anything you have done or can do; it is not a self-created value. You are of great value because that's who our loving God created you to be. Humility is knowing who you are and who made you who you are and giving God the glory. Your value cannot be determined by other people—not even yourself. Only your Creator can determine the value of his creation.

## You Are Lovable

The Bible speaks repeatedly and powerfully of how much you are loved. For example:

> Jesus prayed to his Father, "You love them as much as you love me" (John 17:23 NLT).
> *God loves you as much as he loves Jesus.*

> Jesus says to his followers, "As the Father has loved me, so have I loved you. Now remain in my love" (John 15:9).
> *Jesus loves you as much as God the Father loves Jesus.*

> The Bible says to us, "See what great love the Father has lavished on us, that we should be called children of God! And that is what we are!" (1 John 3:1).
> *God loves you so much, he made you his own son or daughter.*

> God's Word declares, "He who did not spare his own Son, but gave him up for us all—how will he not also, along with him, graciously give us all things?" (Romans 8:32).
> *God loves you so much, he gave everything for you.*

You may have grown up feeling ignored, unwanted, despised, or even hated. The people who conveyed that image to you were in error. God created you in his image and loves you as his own child. God makes no mistakes. If he loves you—and he does—you are eternally lovable. It is essential that you see yourself as lovable because that is how God sees you.

Jesus didn't endure rejection, ridicule, torture, and death for the sake of trash. In love, he went to the cross to redeem and restore a relationship with that which was lost—you. One of the most well-known verses in Scripture shows how great his love for you is, "For God so loved the world, that he gave his one and only Son . . ." (John 3:16). God doesn't merely tolerate or love you as a result of Christ's work on the cross. Rather, his love was the fuel that sent Jesus to the cross for you.

See how Psalm 17:8 expresses God's love and affection toward us. It says, "Keep me as the apple of your eye; hide me in the shadow of your wings." At face value, this may not seem to carry much weight. But the Hebrew word for "apple" literally means "little man." When you stand close enough to someone, you see a tiny reflection of yourself in that person's pupil. You see yourself as the "apple" of his or her eye. In this psalm, David is saying this is who you are to God. You are the "little man" reflected in God's eye. You are always in his vision. You are always the object of his affection and obsession. This is how much you are loved and valued.

## You Are Unique

No one in the world has ever or will ever be you. Your uniqueness exceeds your race, culture, personality, physical features, likes, dislikes, gifts and talents, and the way God wired you. You display God's image in a way no one else can or ever will. The Bible even refers to you as "God's masterpiece" (Ephesians 2:10 NLT). What the ancient songwriter sang to God about himself is true also of you: "For you created my inmost being; you knit me together in my mother's womb. I praise you because I am fearfully and wonderfully made; your works are wonderful, I know that full well" (Psalm 139:13–14). As a potter creates a beautiful and unique piece of art with his clay, taking time to mold it, shape it, and sculpt it, so God did with you (see Isaiah 64:8).

God made you with unique gifts and talents that are crucial to this world. 1 Corinthians 12 refers to Christians, corporately, as "the body of Christ," and the analogy is drawn between how a physical body functions and how the body of Christ functions. The passage makes it clear that each of us, whatever our race, personality, gifts, and talents may be, is unique, crucial, and significant:

> The eye cannot say to the hand, "I don't need you!" And the head cannot say to the feet, "I don't need you!" On the contrary, those parts of the body that seem to be weaker are indispensable, and the parts that we think are less honorable we treat with special honor. And the parts that are unpresentable are treated with special modesty, while our presentable parts need no special treatment. But God has put the body together, giving greater honor to the parts that lacked it, so that there should be no division in the body, but that its parts should have equal concern for each other. If one part suffers, every part suffers with it; if one part is honored, every part rejoices with it.
>
> Now you are the body of Christ, and each one of you is a part of it. (1 Corinthians 12:21–27)

You are unique, crucial, and significant. You are here for a purpose. The world is better because of you. We all need you to know your value, understand how much you're loved, and embrace the things that make you *you*.

## The Outflow of Embracing Your True Self

One day I (Josh) boarded a plane and saw something strange. The female flight attendant who was greeting the boarding passengers was holding a dozen beautiful roses. I have been on literally thousands of commercial flights, but I have never before seen a flight attendant holding a bouquet of flowers.

I stopped and said to her, "Did your boyfriend bring you those flowers?"

"No," she said.

"Your husband, then?"

She shook her head.

"Well, then," I pressed, "who did?"

"I bought them for myself," she said, smiling broadly.

I went back to my seat and stowed my carry-on bags, then I went back up front and introduced myself to the flight attendant. During our conversation, I indicated that I was in Christian ministry, and she told me that she was also a believer.

Still curious about the flowers, I said, "Why did you buy yourself a dozen roses?"

She answered immediately. "Because I like myself."

I thought, *That's incredible.* So, I went and bought myself *two* dozen roses.

What a tremendous platform that woman had for sharing Christ with others, and what a great testimony she had. How we perceive ourselves can make all the difference in the effectiveness of our living and spoken witness. As we grow in the awareness that God loves us, values us, and is using us, we become what Paul called "the fragrance of life" to those who are desperately searching for the peace we enjoy as God's children (see 2 Corinthians 2:16).

God has a greater purpose for restoring our faulty self-portrait, even more than overcoming our unwanted behaviors and struggles. He wants us to be utterly convinced that we are loved, valuable, and competent because he has work for us to do. Do you realize that you and I are God's gift to the world? If not, we have no reason to be here. It would have made more sense for God to take us straight up to heaven the moment we trusted Christ. God has a mission for us—to share his message of love, forgiveness, and reconciliation to himself and invite others into a personal relationship with their Creator.

Our Christian training has drummed into many of us that we ought to share Christ with others. For those of us who do not have a clear sense of who we are as God's loved, valued, and competent children, the challenge to witness only produces greater guilt as the years pass by and we don't see anyone come to faith in

Christ because of us. In fact, the inner self-portrait seems even more distorted because we suspect that God loves us less for our lack of fruitfulness as his witnesses. But God wants us to have a thriving relationship with him and others, to see him as he truly is and ourselves as he sees us, and to enjoy his goodness because then others will be attracted to and convinced by the thriving life of freedom and maximum satisfaction that he created us for.

Maybe it's time for you to buy a dozen roses as a moment of declaration that you are going to embrace who God created you to be, thank him for what he has done, and love the world around you. Maybe it's time to "treat yo self" by getting a painting or portrait to put on your wall to remind you to see yourself as God sees you. Maybe it's time to find ways to celebrate how much God values you, loves you, and wants to use you and your unique contributions to the world.

## Becoming Who You Already Are

Many of us may resonate with these truths of who we are, but struggle to believe them due to our unmet longings, painful experiences, and the negative core beliefs we have developed over many years. Seeing ourselves as God sees us is one of the most important factors in overcoming unwanted behaviors. A rich confidence and trust in God to meet our longings develops a resilience, a resistance to the need to cope through unwanted behaviors. When we know who we are and have positive biblical core beliefs about ourselves, we separate our unmet longings from our identity and seek their fulfillment in healthy ways.

So how do we experience this change in ourselves? Well, we can't change—not exactly. The authors of *The Cure* explain:

> The goal is not to change me. I'm already changed. The goal is to mature. When I depend on the new creature I've been made into through the work of Jesus at the cross, I begin to

live healthier, more free of sin, more free to love. I learn to believe all His power, love, truth, and goodness already exists in me, right now. Even on my worst day.[5]

We have already been transformed at the moment of salvation, after which we grow and mature into who Christ has made us. Our spiritual activity will never transform our spiritual identity. This suggests that we who follow Jesus have already been changed by his power at work in us, and now it is a matter of our hearts, thoughts, and behaviors lining up more and more with what is already true of us.

This doesn't mean we just sit back and become complacent with our unwanted behaviors and issues. No, we strive, get help, and play an active role in the maturing process (1 Corinthians 15:10). Jesus talked about taking drastic measures to deal with sin in our lives (Matthew 5:29). The beauty, though, is that we struggle not to *change* our identity; we strive *from* a changed identity. We don't try to become something new, but because we are something new we make every effort to experience the joy, peace, and satisfaction of the life we were created to live.

As you live according to and grow into who God has already made you to be, it will take a conscious effort to remember your true identity. You are not unlovable. You are not worthless. You are not the sum of what people have said or done to you. You are made in the image of God with infinite dignity and value, and you are loved. You're not defined by what you've done to someone, by what you've done to yourself, or by what's been done to you. You're defined by God and the identity he has given you as his beloved son or daughter. Rest in your value as an image bearer and your identity as a son or daughter who has been adopted into God's family. Seek relationships that fulfill your Seven Longings and people who affirm your true value as a child of God. Dwell on who God says you are and how much he values you. Meditate on times in life where you have felt his love and experienced his acceptance.

Whenever you feel inadequate, unloved, or like just another face in the crowd, begin asking what lie you're returning to or what untruth you're believing about yourself. Then take that lie captive and tell yourself who you truly are. For a step-by-step process to do this, incorporating research from neuroscience, check out Renewing the Mind in the appendix of this book.

## Questions for Reflection

1. Do you at times view yourself as either worthless, unlovable, or just a face in the crowd?
2. What unmet longings and painful experiences from the past may have led you to develop those negative core beliefs about yourself?
3. What positive core belief(s) about your true identity do you want to grow in believing?
4. Do you know anyone with whom you can intentionally spend time—someone who treats you as valuable, loved, and unique?

# CHAPTER NINE

# YOU'RE MADE FOR MORE

I remember it like it was yesterday. I (Josh) had buried a secret for a long time that I knew I needed to share with my wife, Dottie. At that time we had been married twenty-five years. I asked her if we could talk, so we sat down on the carpet in our living room. It was hard to get the words out.

For the second time in my life, I was going to share with someone else my story of being sexually abused as a little boy. Trembling, I told her. "When I was a boy, from ages 6–13 years old, I was sexually abused, raped, and forced to look at homosexual pornography by Wayne Bailey, the hired hand on our family farm." She immediately grabbed me, hugged me tightly, looked deeply into my eyes and said, "Honey! I am so sorry this happened to you. It's a good thing he's no longer alive or he'd have to deal with me! I love you so much!"

I felt relieved, accepted, and totally loved. She thanked me for sharing this, and then gently said something I never could have anticipated. She said, "I so appreciate you trusting me with your story. I am so proud of you, and so sorry you had to go through all of this. But, Josh, this is a profound message, and if you want to share it with the whole world, I will firmly support you, because so many people have had to deal with this anguish and need to hear your story!" I was stunned. That was the last reaction I could have anticipated. It was contrary to her very private personality.

That experience with Dottie and her words of acceptance and encouragement were exactly what I needed. It was one of the most impactful and positive experiences of my life.

Dottie was the second person I had told this part of my story. The first was my mother. Around age eleven, I finally had the courage to tell her that, for the last five years, I had been sexually abused by Wayne Bailey. I needed her to believe and protect me, but she didn't. Not only that, but she whipped me until I was forced to scream that I was lying. That was the darkest moment of my life.

The physical wounds from that beating healed, but emotionally I felt rejected, afraid, and angry about that agonizing part of my life. I felt alone and disconnected. I didn't feel that I could share that with anyone else, ever again, so I buried that secret for the next forty years. I never lied about it; I just kept the details hidden, fearing further rejection. But as much as my mom's response caused fear and alienation, Dottie's reaction communicated unconditional acceptance and love. I can honestly say, and Dottie would agree, that after I shared all of my story with her, our connection and emotional intimacy grew.

## How We Thrive

What do you believe grows people most? I have asked this question to many and heard countless answers. We believe that relationships grow people the most. As explored in this book so far, all relationships fall into three categories—relationship with God, relationship with self, and relationships with others. In this chapter, we'll dive deeper into the third relationship category. Our relationships with other people form the rich soil for us to experience greater spiritual and emotional wholeness. That is, others have the ability to show us God's love and model his character. They have the ability to love and accept us, helping us to know and believe our true value and identity.

When we have healthy relationships with God, ourselves, and others in place in our lives, we begin to thrive because this is how we were designed. You were created to thrive. You were created to have your Seven Longings met in healthy ways, and when this happens you will thrive. You can then start operating out of healthy core beliefs about yourself, God, and others.

Why is this the case? We were created by a relational God. We were made to be fully known and fully loved. We were made to love, serve, support, and show the love of God to others. We need others and others need us. We are relational, and relational wholeness is what furthers and supports our spiritual and emotional wholeness. And, as we are wounded in our relationships with others, we must be healed in our relationships with others.

## Relational Wholeness from a Relational God

What was the first crisis in human history? Many would point to Adam and Eve eating from the tree in Genesis 3:6—the entrance of sin into the world. This was a crisis, certainly, but it was not the first. The first crisis occurred in the previous chapter, Genesis 2, which records the words of God: "It is not good for the man to be alone" (Genesis 2:18). It was a crisis of aloneness. Didn't Adam have God right there with him? Yes, of course; God was with him in the garden, but God himself observed that Adam was alone. Adam had fellowship with God, but there was no one just like him to live life with. One commentator writes, "God has created human life to have fellowship with him but also to be a social entity, building relationships with other human beings."[1] God's words in Genesis 2 make a statement about Adam's aloneness that reveals to us part of who God is and what it means to be made in his image.

In the last chapter we shared about emotional wholeness. We are made in the image of God, which means we have inherent dignity and value. We can overcome shame and develop healthy core beliefs about ourselves. But there is another dimension to being made in the image of God that we call relational wholeness, or the completeness that comes from experiencing healthy relationships with others. You were made by a relational God for healthy relationships.

Relationship is and always will be at the core of who God is. In both the Old and New Testaments, the Bible teaches that God is a Trinity. God exists as three persons, yet he is one being. Each person—the Father, the Son, and the Holy Spirit—has a separate identity while enjoying the same essence of nature as the others, not merely similar natures in different roles. Some might think this is confusing or contradictory. But the Bible's depiction of God as one God who eternally coexists as three persons conveys an amazing truth, showing us that intimate relationship has existed eternally. God didn't create humans because he needed a relationship; he already had relationship. He exists in relationship. The Father has always infinitely loved the Son, the Son has always infinitely loved the Father, and the Holy Spirit has always infinitely loved both the Father and the Son. A continuous cycle of perfect relationships is experienced within the Godhead. While we are unable to fully comprehend such a perfect and continuing relationship, all of us long to experience this kind of relationship ourselves. The image of God can be fully seen in us only through relationships.

Relationships are part of our core identity. God said, "It is not good for the man to be alone." He made humans in his image, and that image reflected the perfect relationship of the three persons of the Godhead: an infinitely loving oneness, a bonding, a togetherness, and a connectedness unparalleled in the universe.

And he desired for his human creation a oneness similar to his. So, instead of leaving his newly created man alone, he made another human from the man's side—Eve.

Just as God is in relationship by his very nature, so he creates us to be in relationship. God's unity in the Trinity is the key that unlocks how our relationships are meant to work. While we can never comprehend God's oneness in relationship in an absolute sense, we can gain enough insight into this mystery to experience the true meaning of relationship. Uncovering the mystery of the Trinity is like peering into the very heart of God.

Nothing in life can make more of an impact on you than a human relationship, or the lack of it. We are hardwired for relationship and connection from the time we are born; indeed, we can't even survive initially, let alone thrive, without human relationships. The opposite of thriving is living in isolation and disconnection from others. No thriving person is isolated and disconnected, and no isolated and disconnected person is thriving.

## Human Connection: Surviving & Thriving

How important is human connection? Much research has been done on the importance of the role of a primary caregiver, which is typically a parent. One of the most famous studies is known today as the Still Face Experiment,[2] which paired infants with a primary caregiver. The adult would play face-to-face with the child, without toys, for three minutes before turning away momentarily and then looking back at the infant. Next, the caregiver was instructed to remain completely unresponsive, maintaining eye contact but making no facial expressions, for two minutes. Then the caregiver resumed play as before for three minutes.

The results were striking (you can watch videos of the experiment online). The moment the caregiver turns away and becomes unresponsive, the babies immediately feel the shift from connection to disconnection, responsive play to unresponsive stare.

Within the two "still face" minutes, the infants seem desperate to reconnect and get a response from the caregiver. They reach out, point, cry, scream, and kick. The disconnection and unresponsiveness throws the infant into a flurry of anxiety and distress, until the caregiver re-engages in play and reconnects with the child.

The Still Face Experiment reveals how important connection and relationship are to us as humans—and how destructive even two minutes of disconnection can be. God made us as relational beings, and our need for connection with others is apparent from the earliest moments of childhood. And, biblically speaking, our relationships—with God and others—are among the few things that endure beyond this life.

## Relational Brokenness & Wholeness

Relationships are the birthplace of both beauty and brokenness. We are blessed by relationships when they are healthy and hurt by them when they're not (and even the best relationships can still hurt us). When we are hurt in relationships, we need to be healed in them by having our Seven Longings met in healthy ways.

Each of us was made to be fully known and fully loved within a relationship, both with God and with others. Like God, who in the Trinity is the ultimate example of three persons being fully known and fully loved, we were created with an inborn need to be fully known and fully loved. Since God is omniscient, meaning he knows all things (see John 21:17), he knows everything about each of us. He knows all of our secrets, thoughts, hurts, and longings. He knows all and still wants an intimate and personal relationship with us (see Romans 5:8).

Not only are we fully known by God, we are also fully loved when we are reconciled to God through a saving relationship with Jesus. The longing to be fully known and fully loved is met in our relationship with God, but just like Adam in the Garden we are also made to be fully known and fully loved by other people.

Timothy and Kathy Keller have written:

To be loved but not known is comforting but superficial. To be known and not loved is our greatest fear. But to be fully known and truly loved is, well, a lot like being loved by God. . . . It liberates us from pretense, humbles us out of our self-righteousness, and fortifies us for any difficulty life can throw at us.[3]

Deep within we crave being fully known, yet we also fear it. If you are intentionally holding onto hurts, secret sin, or unwanted behaviors and telling someone almost-but-not-quite everything, that is the Enemy's playground for shame, lies, and disconnection. Here's what happens: Someone gives you a compliment or treats you with respect or shows appreciation to you—actions that could fill one of your Seven Longings—but you dismiss it. You can't receive it. You think, *If they* really *knew me they wouldn't do that.* Their words are filtered through the things you're holding back from them. The secrets you can't tell hold you captive, because only the parts you allow to be truly known can be fully loved.

Being fully known is challenging. It requires sharing the guilt and shame you bear in life due to the sins you have committed against others (and yourself), as well as those sins that have been done to you. But remember, there is a difference between guilt and shame. Guilt says, "I did bad." Shame says, "I am bad." Rejection and shame are the primary factors that keep people from sharing all of themselves with others. The only way to get back to healthy connection is by taking the risk of being fully known.

Dr. Ted Roberts once told me, "What we need the most is what we fear the most." The cost of what we need the most is high; it's hard for everyone and it never gets easier. But it may be the most powerful tool you'll ever discover; it's called vulnerability. Researcher and author Brené Brown defines vulnerability as "uncertainty, risk, and emotional exposure."[4] Scary stuff.

But Brené also says that "vulnerability is the birthplace of love, belonging, joy, courage, empathy, and creativity."[5]

Jessica was a college student who had been addicted to hardcore pornography since she was a teen. She had tried everything she knew how to get free. She prayed, read the Bible, was involved in church, and truly loved Jesus. But she felt alone. She struggled in silence. She was so filled with guilt and shame she could barely live inside her own skin. She knew she needed to be vulnerable enough to ask for help, but she had always been told that porn was a male issue, so she felt like a freak. She feared being judged or rejected. When she was finally caught, she felt relief until the supervisor who found hardcore pornography in her browsing history dismissed the discovery, saying, "We know this wasn't you; women just don't have this problem." Jessica was devastated and felt like she would never be able to share her problem with anyone.

Many dark months passed before hope broke through. Jessica transferred to a Bible college where the female resident life leaders talked openly and honestly about pornography and sexual sin to the new female students and invited them to be vulnerable about their struggles. Jessica wrote a note about her struggle with pornography and handed it to one of the leaders. Soon a woman in leadership came to her, told her she had taken a brave step in being vulnerable, and outlined the steps they could take to help. Fear had kept Jessica captive to isolation and disconnection, the very place she could never find freedom. Only by being fully seen and known in her pain, struggle, and sin could she be met with the love and connection that helped her walk into the wholeness and freedom for which God made her.

People have asked me, "Josh, why didn't you tell your story of being sexually abused from the start?" There are many reasons, but here are the main two. First, I didn't want to share and be known around the world only as a survivor of sexual abuse. That is part of my story, but it's not all of my story, and I feared that people would think of nothing or little else when they thought of me. Second, I was afraid I wouldn't be believed. It took so much courage for me to share my story with my mother that first time; I can't tell you how much I just needed her to believe me and do anything to help. I can't tell you all the negative beliefs that came from not being believed and how much fear affected parts of my life for decades to come. I felt stupid for telling her, and I never wanted to feel that way again. I can understand why it takes so many victims and survivors so long to share their stories, because it is so scary to be fully known with what feels like so much baggage. It is tempting to minimize it and act as if it never happened. But I'm so thankful I finally let Dottie, my family, close friends, and then the world know all of me. I now feel freer and more connected than ever, and it all started with vulnerability. I learned that God's power is not always seen in what he prevents; it can also be seen in the way he takes the broken pieces of our lives and makes something beautiful out of them.

One part of being fully known for me meant sharing what I was most afraid to share. The thing I feared the most, being vulnerable and letting people see this part of me, was the very thing I needed the most to heal. I was wounded in my relationship with my mother and needed to be healed in other relationships that God provided with Dottie, family, and friends.

This process started with me stepping into vulnerability in order to let my whole self be seen and loved by others. As I have met leaders and people from all over the world, I realize that many fear being truly loved and truly loving another. I have met many that have become unwilling to be vulnerable and thus closed themselves off from the love that others have to offer. In his book *The Four Loves*, C. S. Lewis says:

> To love at all is to be vulnerable. Love anything, and your heart will certainly be wrung and possibly be broken. If you want to make sure of keeping it intact, you must give it to

no one, not even to an animal. Wrap it carefully round with hobbies and little luxuries; avoid all entanglements; lock it up safe in the casket or coffin of your selfishness. But in that casket—safe, dark, motionless, airless—it will change. It will not be broken; it will become unbreakable, impenetrable, irredeemable.[6]

To be fully known and fully loved is one of the most rewarding journeys the human heart can take. To be fully known and fully loved is something only God can do perfectly for us, but we, as people made in his image, get to enjoy the life-changing blessings of allowing ourselves to be fully known and fully loved. When we open up to this knowledge and love, we will begin to thrive in ways we never imagined were possible.

## Growth Environments

British journalist Johann Hari made headlines in recent years due to his TED Talk, where he shared "The opposite of addiction is not sobriety. The opposite of addiction is connection."[7] Hari witnessed firsthand the chaos of compulsive and unwanted behaviors with loved ones. This led him on a journey of research and discovery into proven treatment models for those struggling with these behaviors. Johann discovered that addiction was less about the high from the drug, smartphone, behavior, etc., than it was about the inability of individuals to get their needs met through healthy connection with others.[8] These findings are undoubtedly consistent with the biblical concepts we've explored in this book about unmet longings, unwanted behaviors, and returning to healthy relationships with God, self, and others.

How do some of the core concepts of this book play out practically? How do we begin to grow and engage in relationships that help us experience and live according to our identity as sons and daughters of God, being fully known and truly loved? It involves finding—and, when necessary, creating—growth environments that foster spiritual, emotional, and relational wholeness. What does this ideal growth environment look like?

*First, a growth environment will include people who model the truth about who you are in Christ and how much you are loved and valued.* Whom do you spend time with? Are your primary relationships constructive—or at least conducive—to helping you become more aware of who you truly are? You need to spend quality time and quantity time with people who know (and help you know) that you are loved, valued, and useful to God and others, people who love and accept you for who you are, not what you can do. These people will not necessarily be the busiest people for God. Christian "workaholics" are often overly busy because they are trying to earn God's approval instead of confidently walking in it. Good role models of a true sense of identity radiate an intimate relationship with God and genuinely enjoy serving him. These models may or may not be gifted with social skills, but they're comfortable around people because they're confident about their identity. Many of these people are involved in discipleship or mentoring other believers either formally or informally.

*Second, a growth environment is one in which the truth about God and your value is clearly taught from the Scriptures and modeled.* Here, an accurate view of God as your loving Father and your true identity is taught to you. This is not only taught to you by others; it is also modeled to you by others. Perhaps when you were a child you had a parent, teacher, or another significant adult communicate to you that you weren't good enough. That information about who you are is inaccurate. You need to be taught the truth about how God sees you. You need to be around Bible teachers, Bible study leaders, and other mature Christians who declare through their lessons and conversations your acceptance and worth in God's eyes.

*Third, a growth environment provides a context of loving, intimate relationships.* As believers model the truth, you will observe people regarding one another as lovable, valuable, and competent. As believers teach the truth, you will learn from Scripture that God sees you as lovable, valuable, and competent. But as you relate to people who understand their true identity, you will experience this truth personally. It is in the context of caring Christian relationships that people express love to one another, value one another, and serve one another in practical ways.

For example, say that just before you leave work for the day, your boss calls you in and announces that you are being passed over for the promotion and raise you were expecting. A new employee with advanced training has been given priority. Driving home, you're filled with disappointment. Old feelings of inadequacy and failure tempt you to skip your Bible study group that evening; you would rather crawl into a hole and wallow in self-pity. But you've learned to push against negative beliefs about yourself, so you go. You tell your Bible study friends about your misfortune, and they respond by surrounding you with comfort and care. You know their love is genuine because you've been vulnerable with them and they've supported you and encouraged you in the past (and you've done the same for many of them). They remind you that you are still capable, skilled, and useful, not only to the company for which you work, but also to the group. Then during the study, one of the group members mentions the portion of Scripture that depicts God's people as useful—even indispensable—members of Christ's body. Another in the group reminisces about the time you helped his family move into a new apartment. They affirm your spiritual gift of service to others. You leave the group knowing that the glory and beauty of who God has made you has been seen and experienced. You feel loved, appreciated, and needed in the group. The nurturing relationships in that growth environment help you to see clearly that you are a person of worth, usefulness, and purpose to God and others.

# God's Plan for Your Growth

Unfortunately, we will be tempted to return to our unwanted behaviors, to isolate, and to give up on the growth process. What do we do, then? We need an environment where people support us. This type of environment involves a daily choice of reaching out for help, within a safe community, to process the pain and stresses that drive our thinking and behaviors. We recognize that we don't just fall into our unhealthy choices; we go through recurring patterns and cycles before ending back in the places we swore we'd never go to again. We react to challenges, criticism, and stress, and start believing lies and feeling emotions like anger, sadness, or fear. We then begin thinking of ways to cope with or escape these emotions (these cycles of trigger and response often operate at a subconscious level; they have been ingrained in us, leading to fixed brain pathways that we must intentionally reprogram).

What we need is *help in those moments* when our reactive thinking and emotions begin. We need support, encouragement, and love to grow and overcome unhealthy choices. Fortunately, God has given us an incredible gift through the body of Christ to do life together in a much deeper way than we often do. Instead of returning to our unwanted behaviors, which release dopamine in our brains that leads to a momentary good feeling, we can reach out to others for connection, which releases the same "feel good" chemical.[9] By renewing our minds, we get the same thing from healthy connection that we've previously experienced from unhealthy and unwanted behaviors.

Healing begins for us when we develop a lifestyle of reaching out rather than acting out. We have the option of experiencing health and healing as we live openly with safe people. Doing so helps us to understand why we return to destructive behaviors and helps us to steer ourselves well to prevent future harmful choices.

*Again, healing begins for us when we develop a lifestyle of reaching out rather than acting out.*

I (Ben) stayed trapped for years in porn addiction, a food addiction, deep anger, and a multitude of other struggles as I practiced reactive and unhealthy accountability rather than proactive and healing support. Sure, I had internet-filtering software on my devices and an "accountability partner," but this often just resulted in a weekly meeting with a friend to confess my slip-ups after living in isolation for another week. The conversation frequently ended with a commitment to try harder. It was a step toward connection to confess my sin to others (as we are told to do in James 5:16), *but I was seriously limiting my growth by having only weekly interactions to help me gain healing.*

Trying to stop unhealthy choices without first uncovering the *why* behind our actions severely limits our growth. And I was fighting the wrong battles. I focused primarily on my behavior and sin avoidance, rather than seeking healing and *support* for the underlying shame, emotional wounds, and unresolved areas in my life that were at the root of my behaviors. To overcome these, I had *to invite Jesus and others in every day* to help me discern why I struggled and to understand the unresolved areas of my heart and mind that needed healing. Only then could I stop living reactively and experience healing and fulfillment.

In doing so, I discovered that my anger was fueled by the deep, gnawing fear that grew out of the frequent rejection I experienced as a kid from friends and family. I had learned to protect myself with anger, which grew worse in adulthood. And simply trying harder to stop being angry only intensified my struggle.

With the support of others, I assessed the precursors, stressors, emotions, and situations that tended to occur before I "fell into" unwanted behaviors. This involved creating a plan of action with safe people. It meant asking trusted friends to encourage and support me with specific challenges I faced throughout the week. And it helped immensely to learn—and eventually know— that I wouldn't face condemnation but would be met with grace and truth.

This type of support is about inviting others to help us understand why we do what we do, and to help us process the difficulties in life that trigger us to cope. It requires a proactive, daily choice. It aligns with the instruction in 1 John 1:7, which tells us to walk in the light, having fellowship with others and being cleansed from all sin by Jesus. It is a daily lifestyle of being fully transparent with Jesus and safe people about our emotional well-being and struggles.

We do not just "let go and let God." We have been given an active role to play in addressing issues in our lives through the power of the Holy Spirit (see Romans 8:13). As we confess our sins to God and one another, sharing our hurts and struggles and asking for help, the Holy Spirit brings about growth and healing in our lives.

Proactive and healing support is not behavior modification. It is a process of inviting God and others to be part of healing the underlying hurts and unresolved areas of our stories that we'd rather avoid—a major objective of the *Resolution Movement* we've mentioned in this book.[10] It's easier to blame our old sinful nature than to admit that we may be carrying hurt and unresolved shame that keeps us returning to unhealthy patterns. Proactive and healing support is also not limited to simply talking about sin or unhealthy choices in our lives. It's a *daily* lifestyle of reaching out for help to process the pain and stress in life that often influences the ways we try to cope. We must understand that our sin and unhealthy choices are not random. We sin because we are born sinful, but we also sin because we have been sinned against and have developed ways to cope when that past pain gets triggered. When we are proactive and gain healing support, Jesus matures us into who he created us to be.

When we stop fighting the wrong battles and start implementing proactive and healing support, we can invite Jesus to do his greatest work in the rich soil through which he has designed healing and growth to take place. He helps us to overcome struggles and our unwanted behaviors. I know this because he's done it with me.

When you encounter an "activating event"—a situation in which you're tempted to turn to an unwanted behavior—take a moment to "press pause" and walk through a process like the following:

1. Identify the negative sensation you're feeling (e.g., is it rejection? feeling unappreciated? etc.).
2. Acknowledge the God-given longing that underlies that sensation (e.g., if you're feeling rejected, you're feeling an unmet longing for acceptance. Or, if you're feeling insecure in some way, the God-given longing that's being threatened or unfulfilled is the longing for the assurance of safety and security).
3. Counter the negative core beliefs you might be telling yourself with the truth (e.g., "I'm feeling worthless and inadequate, but God says I am of great worth in his sight—and people who know me agree with God on that point").
4. Seek the fulfillment of that longing in healthy ways, such as expressing your need to a trusted friend or group of friends (e.g., "I'm feeling devalued because of some things that happened today; I think I could use some reminders that who I am and what I do is appreciated").
5. Repeat the process as often as necessary.

These few steps, repeated quickly and often when you experience an activating event, can re-program your heart and mind to choose wholeness rather than brokenness. The process can be diagrammed as follows:

## BROKENNESS VS. WHOLENESS

### ACTIVATING EVENT

Any situation that leads to an unmet longing. E.g., rejection from a friend;
thinking about an upcoming task or deadline; a spouse or friend being
unattentive or angry; feeling misunderstood in a conversation.

### UNMET LONGING

The activating event leads to one or more of the Seven
Longings going unmet. This often brings with it the pain of the
same longings going unmet in past circumstances.

| REINFORCE NEGATIVE CORE BELIEFS | REINFORCE POSITIVE CORE BELIEFS |
|---|---|
| Telling yourself lies (e.g., "No one cares," "I am not good enough," "I will never get things right," "I must get revenge," "God isn't good or loving," etc.). | Telling yourself truth (e.g., "I am not defined by their rejection, opinions, or these feelings; I am loved, worthy, redeemed by Jesus, gifted," etc.). |
|  |  |
| **SEEK FULFILLMENT OF LONGINGS IN UNHEALTHY WAYS** | **SEEK FULFILLMENT OF LONGINGS IN HEALTHY WAYS** |
| Overworking to feel a sense of worth. Over/Undereating to regain control/feel safe. Looking at porn to feel someone's attention. Procrastination, anxiety, depression, oversleeping, anger, etc. | Reach out to safe people and share your unmet longings and feelings. Ask them to remind you of truth. Experience acceptance and validation. Talk to God and meditate on who he says you are. |
|  |  |
| **FURTHER BROKENNESS** | **FURTHER WHOLENESS** |
| Shame, unresolve, loss of control. Remaining stuck in unwanted behaviors and unhealthy patterns. Repeat the cycle. | Satisfaction, healing, resilience. Growing into your true identity and overcoming unhealthy patterns. Repeat the cycle. |

As we take steps toward wholeness, having our longings met, and seeking support from others, we begin to build a rich environment of healing and health. Such an environment can replace the view of yourself you have carried from childhood with the truth of who God has made you and called you to be. It is vital for you to be involved in an ongoing, loving, mutually supportive relationship with other believers. It may be in an adult Sunday school class, a neighborhood Bible study group, or a small group from your church. The group must be small enough that you can get to know a number of people on an intimate level. Merely sitting in a church for a few hours on Sunday morning does not allow for much relationship-building. Find—or help create—a small group where consistent, loving interaction reinforces the truth of who God says you are.

"This process sounds like discipleship," you may say. Yes, the transformation of our sense of identity is wrapped up in the discipleship process. However, we often view discipleship as learning how to live the Christian life. In its broadest sense, rather, discipleship is the process of learning how to be a follower of Jesus. You need to know who you are before you can understand how to live. For many, unfortunately, the discipleship process is derailed or distorted from the beginning because we are so blinded by our unmet longings that we do not believe who God says we are. We have faulty core beliefs that set us up to get trapped in unwanted behaviors. We just try to muster up enough willpower to read our Bibles, share the gospel, serve others more, and so on, while skipping over the wounds and lies that keep us stuck.

God has designed us to heal from hurts, overcome struggles, and thrive in life. He has designed us to grow into the persons he says we are. This can happen as we understand our unmet longings, work through the lies that have taken root, get support from others, and surround ourselves with a rich growth environment.

No matter the hurt you carry, the things you've done, or the lies you believe, God wants you as you are today. Jesus desires to forgive you and heal you. He wants you to experience rich relationships with him and other people. He desires for you to be fully known and fully loved. He wants you to be free to thrive. Will you take the step to be involved in a growth environment, and share with safe people the broken parts of your life and story?

# Questions for Reflection

1. Who is one person you can be vulnerable with to share the areas of your life causing shame?
2. What risks might you face if you continue on in life without being vulnerable and seeking healing?
3. What is the greater vision God might have for your life, to make an impact for him, that is being limited by hurts and unwanted behaviors?
4. What is one step you can take today to get involved in a growth environment?

# CHAPTER TEN

# WHAT'S TRUE FOR ME IS TRUE FOR YOU

Six-year-old Alejandra climbed out of her bedroom window onto the porch roof. She was proudly dressed in her Halloween Supergirl costume. An avid fan of the *Supergirl* TV series, she took one step and a leap forward, just as she had seen her superhero do many times, but not with the same results. Rather than taking off in flight, Alejandra fell to the ground, breaking her leg and fracturing her arm.

Asked why she jumped from the porch roof, Alejandra explained that because she had Supergirl's cape and suit, she believed she would also possess Supergirl's power of flight. But believing didn't make it so. The truth is, humans can't fly like Supergirl, no matter how much a person believes it to be so.

What's true for Alejandra is equally true for you and me. Why? Because humans are not physiologically structured to fly and therefore cannot overcome the universal law of gravity. The fact is certain things in this world are right and true because they conform to reality.

So far in this book, we have demonstrated that we have legitimate needs and longings. When these needs and longings are met in the right ways, we thrive emotionally, relationally, and spiritually. The converse is also true. When our needs and longings go unmet—or when we try to meet them in illegitimate ways—we suffer emotionally, relationally, and spiritually. Why? Because we are not conforming to or living in accordance with the reality of how we were designed to live.

Webster defines truth, in part, as "the body of real things, events, or facts; the property of being in accordance with fact or reality."[1] Flying like the DC Comics character Supergirl isn't in accordance with the known realities of this natural world.

Modern culture has shifted away from an understanding and acknowledgment of objective truth. An objective truth is something that is true for all people, of all cultures, for all time. It is universally true regardless of an individual's experiences or feelings. For example, "humans need water and air to live." That's true for everyone, everywhere, regardless of opinion or emotion. In recent years, however, talking about objective truth is typically viewed as being closed-minded, as more people have become convinced that all truth is subjective—determined solely by the person or persons making the judgment, so that something may be "true" for me and "not true" for you. This has been a radical shift, but even more radical is the prevailing idea today that truth is determined by emotions. If it *feels* true, then it is—for you. Simply put, we live in the first moment in history when feelings are viewed as trumping science and facts.

I recently saw this in full effect in a television interview of author Michael Wolff, who wrote *Fire and Fury* about former U.S. President Donald Trump. MSNBC's Katy Tur asked Wolff a question about the credibility of his book: "If people are questioning it, why not produce the evidence?" Wolff responded, "My evidence is the book. Read the book. If it makes sense to you, if it strikes a chord, if it rings true, it is true." Tur said, "I read it . . . a lot of the stuff did . . . feel true . . ." Wolff claimed that the reader's feelings trumped evidence. He asserted that the truth of his statements and conclusions relied solely on the reader's feelings, and his interviewer seemed to fully accept his reasoning.[2]

This is a cultural shift that is in its third progression. For centuries, the basis of truth was seen as objective: what you observe. The second progression said truth is subjective: what you think. Today, Wolff and others promote a third progression, the idea that truth is emotion: what you feel. Truth is increasingly regarded as something felt rather than something known.

You may wonder who really cares about truth in today's world. The fact is, we all do. Have you ever typed the right address into your phone's mapping app and been taken to the wrong place? It's frustrating, isn't it? We all expect that when we put in the right address, it will take us to the right place. We want our devices to operate according to a reliable standard of truth. In the same way, we want people, ourselves included, to be able to operate according to a truth standard. We all care about things and people fulfilling what is true.

## A Universal Truth

Some today would say that an objective universal moral truth does not exist. They would assert that all moral truth is subjectively determined by personal choice or preference. For example, which statement is true: "Dogs make the best pets" or "Cats make the best pets"? Your answer would depend on your preferences; it would be neither right nor wrong, true nor untrue. Dogs can be the best pet to you, and a cat can be the best pet to me. There is no contradiction in this case because we are talking about our subjective preferences. Such opinion or preference is relative to the individual and can change. But moral truth is another matter because there is such a thing as universal moral truth.

For example, if there is no objective universal moral truth, then the #MeToo movement has no legitimacy. Your value as a person is baseless if there is no universal moral truth. The truths we have explored in this book about who God is, how much you are loved, our need for others, and how our brain gets wired and can heal, would have no bearing. Yet inwardly we know certain things are dead wrong. We know that rape, child abuse, and genocide are wrong. Every person who has suffered under the hand of an abuser "knows" within himself or herself that it is wrong. Such things are not wrong simply because we *feel* they are wrong; we *know* that they are truly, objectively, absolutely wrong.

We can say "what's true for me is true for you" because truth is not a societal or cultural construct. It is not a created concept that can be altered. Truth is rooted in the nature of God. Jesus said, "I am the way and the truth and the life" (John 14:6). We must look to Jesus to find out what truth is. Additionally, every one of us was created in the image and likeness of a relational God. Because of this, we all have an inherent design, as we've seen in this book, that causes us to thrive. We have longings that drive our actions. To say it another way: there is a universal way to wholeness and emotional health because we were created to live in relationship with God and one another—and not just in any kind of relationship, but in relational wholeness that fosters emotional and spiritual wholeness.

Webster goes on to define truth as having "fidelity to an original or standard."[3] That original or standard is determined outside ourselves; it is, by necessity, objective.

Try to build a house using your own standard of measurement. Pour footers haphazardly, cut joists according to your mood of the moment, and nail drywall wherever you like, independently of any code or standard. What kind of house will you build? A house that will not stand.

Construction of a reliable structure conforms to a universal standard of measurement. You don't measure subjectively; you measure objectively. Every measured length, width, and height is in accordance to the universal standard that has been established by the International Bureau of Weights and Measures. When a six-foot-long board matches the six-foot mark on a measuring tape, which in turn conforms to the international standard for six feet, you can truthfully state that it is, in fact, six feet long. It is a correct and true length when it conforms precisely to the original or standard of measurement. When you build a house using objective standards, you're more likely to have a house that will stand.

## The Universal Standard of Truth

What is the standard, then, for universal moral truth? Jesus asserted it when he said, "I am the way and the truth and the life" (John 14:6). He is the one who defines and models emotional, relational, and spiritual wholeness. And it is his Word, the Bible, which communicates that universal moral truth to us.

Universal moral truth isn't simply a preference or an abstract concept; it originates in a person who is the original and abiding standard for morality. Moral truth ultimately finds its source in a "who," not merely in a "what." In other words, moral claims are universally true if they correspond to the character of God, who is the objective source for morality. God is the Source of all moral truth. "He is the Rock," Moses said, "his work is perfect . . . a God of truth and without iniquity, just and right is he" (Deuteronomy 32:4 KJV). God's nature and character determine moral truth. He defines what is right and wrong, good and evil. But truth is not first and foremost something he decides; it is something he *is*.

The basis of everything we call moral, the Source of every good thing, is the eternal God who is outside us, above us, and beyond us. The apostle James wrote, "Every good and perfect gift is from above, coming down from the Father of the heavenly lights, who does not change like shifting shadows" (James 1:17).

The reason we have this concept that some things are morally right and others are morally wrong is not because a church prop-agates it or even that it is written in a book called the Bible. The moral authority of the Bible isn't found in its commands and rules. The authority of Scripture is derived directly from and founded in the very character and nature of God and represented in the flesh through Jesus Christ. All moral truth resides in and comes from God.

The reason we think that there are such concepts as "fair" and "unfair" is because our Maker is a just God.

The reason honesty is right and deceit is wrong is because God is true.

The reason other-focused love is right and selfishness is wrong is because the God of relationships who formed us is a God of love.

Everything that is moral, right, and good flows from the nature of God. He directs us to follow in his ways, because his ways lead us down a path of wholeness and thriving. And when we see God as the source of all moral truth, it affects how we see the rules and laws that he gives us.

It may make sense to say we were created by a relational God, in his image, and are designed to enjoy thriving and fulfilling relationships. But how do we know this? How can we be confident that God exists, that he has shown up in the person of Jesus Christ, and that the Bible that declares all this is a trustworthy source?

## Where the Evidence Points

Nineteen years old. Arrogant. Skeptical. Determined. That de-scribed me (Josh) as I left college in the United States and traveled to Europe to do research in an attempt to disprove the claims of Christianity. Specifically, I intended to show that the Bible was historically unreliable, and that Jesus was not the Son of God.

Standing in the Glasgow University library in Scotland, I stared at an ancient New Testament manuscript. It was a fragment from John 16, and the ink and papery substance on which it was written were more than 1,600 years old. This rare, third-century, handwritten portion of the Gospel of John was housed under a protective glass case in the university library. It was a priceless artifact that quoted Jesus.

A strange and unexpected feeling washed over me as I stood there. Though at the time I couldn't read or understand a single line of the Greek in which that manuscript was written, these words seemed to reach out to me in an almost mystical way. And though I wasn't a Christian at the time, I sensed an uncanny power in these words.

Gazing at these ancient manuscripts, I was far from humble. My arrogance had gotten the better of me. I was out to prove to a group of Christian students that their faith in Christ and the Bible was both foolish and unfounded. When I scoffed at them, they challenged me to examine the evidence for the reliability of the Bible and the claims of Jesus Christ. I accepted that challenge in pride, and my journey began right there in Glasgow.

I made my way from the libraries and museums of Scotland to the English libraries of Cambridge, Oxford, and Manchester. I examined and studied the ancient manuscripts housed there, including the earliest known manuscripts, at the time, of the New Testament. I spent months researching at universities in Germany, France, and Switzerland. After devouring dozens of books and speaking with leading scholars, I ended up at the Evangelical Library on Chiltern Street in London. It was about 6:30 in the evening when I pushed aside the many books that were gathered around me. Leaning back in my chair, I stared up at the ceiling and spoke these words aloud without even thinking: "It's true!" I repeated them two more times. "It's true. It really is true!"

A flood of emotions swept over me as I realized that the biblical record of Christ's life, death, and resurrection was recorded accurately and was in fact true. The truth that Christ was God's Son penetrated deep into my soul. I could no longer reject the reality of Christ and be intellectually honest with myself. The impact of that realization was truly a defining moment for me. I recognized that I was not rejecting Christ for any intellectual reasons, but for emotional reasons. I had been wrestling with the question, "Is the Bible true?," but what I was really wrestling with was, "Is who the Bible is about good?" and "How could God be good if he allowed me to be sexually abused and be hurt so much?" I was slowly coming to understand who God really was. The love and acceptance I felt from my Christian friends at university, who had encouraged me to investigate the credibility of Christianity, was revealing how much Jesus loved me. I soon came to grips with my rebellion and rejection of Christianity. I began to see that my sin and wrongdoing was standing between me and a loving God who had sent his Son to die in my place. The power and profound meaning of these ancient manuscripts brought me face-to-face with the truth. And the truth was a Person. And his name was Jesus.

I would soon pray and trust in Christ as my personal Savior. That relationship changed me from the inside out and launched me into a journey with Christ that has led me to a life of thriving and wholeness, the life I was created for.

I have spent most of my life since that moment researching and sharing the evidences for the truth of Jesus's claims, the reality of his bodily resurrection, and the reliability of the Scriptures that testify to the truth. I have authored dozens of books to reinforce our faith in God and his Word that gives us a universal moral truth to live by. And I've discovered that more often than not, people's reluctance to consider (let alone be persuaded by) the evidence for the Christian faith relates not to their intellectual misgivings but to the pain and unmet longings in their past. Some blame God (whether they "believe" in him or not) for things that happened to them. Others have been hurt by people who claimed to be followers of Jesus. Still others are reacting to the harmful actions of those who've used the Bible as a weapon rather than the "good news" it proclaims. Their pain is real, and I don't take it lightly. But it makes no sense to call the hurts we've suffered in the past "wrong" or "evil" while simultaneously denying the existence of an objective, universal, and eternal standard of "right" and "good." If we erase God from our thinking and ignore his standards of truth and right-from-wrong, we erode the grounds on which to say, "This shouldn't have happened to me." Good exists because God does; evil is evil because it offends God—and the image of God in us.

Still, I don't expect you to take my word for it. I don't *want* you to take my word for it. I invite you to do as I did and as others have done—as Ben relates later—and investigate the evidence for yourself. I'm fully confident that you'll discover more-than-sufficient evidence that enables us to believe that Jesus is who he claimed to be—the Son of the one true God—and that the Bible is an accurate reflection of what God longs for us to know. I'm glad to say that the Bible's basis for everything we've explored in this book—our Seven Longings, how our unmet longings lead to unwanted behaviors, and how we can heal and thrive—is trustworthy. Ultimately, we can summarize what truth is and isn't, and why, by the following two phrases: 1) That which coincides or reflects the nature or character of God is right (righteous and true). 2) That which does not coincide with or reflect the nature and character of God is false (untrue and unrighteous).

## Who Do You Say I Am?

An overwhelming amount of evidence points to the conclusion that Christianity is true, the Bible is reliable, and God's truth is objective and has bearing on our lives. You may be asking yourself, "So what?" Why is this important? As C. S. Lewis once said, "Christianity, if false, is of no importance, and if true, of infinite importance. The only thing it cannot be is moderately important."[4]

If all of this is true, we can know beyond a shadow of a doubt that the biblical truths in this book are true for each of us: Our value, God's character, our need for others, the effects of our unmet longings, why we get stuck in unwanted behaviors, and how we can return to the thriving life we were designed to live. If all of this is true, then understanding and fulfilling your God-given Seven Longings is of infinite importance. When you know who you are because of who your Creator says you are, and how to relate with the world based on the way he made it and designed it, you will come to know and experience God in profound ways. C. S. Lewis said it this way: "I believe in Christianity as I believe that the sun has risen, not only because I see it but because by it, I see everything else."[5]

But despite having all the evidence in the world, we may still find ourselves holding back. We may still refrain from following Jesus. Sometimes our unmet longings run so deep that we blame God and scoff at the thought of surrendering to him. We make assumptions about his character based on the tragedies we have weathered. You may have wondered if Christianity is true, while doubting at a deeper level whether God is good. And how could he be good, when there is much suffering and evil in the world?

Years before I (Ben) knew Josh personally, I had many doubts stemming from my unmet longings and wounds. As I mentioned previously in this book, I had experienced much rejection, criticism, and judgment from authority figures and, though I didn't know it at the time, I viewed God through the distorted lenses of my hurts rather than the truth. I thought that although I had given my life to Jesus and was a Christian, I was self-deceived and God would reject me when I died. I lived in torment, daily obsessing about dying and going to hell, so I would cry out to God, sometimes twenty times a day, that he would save my soul. I also doubted his existence often and struggled to view him as a loving and close Father.

When I was a freshman in college, these doubts persisted. But there I met other students who were crazy about Jesus. They exuded his love. They accepted and loved me, flaws and all. They wanted to be around me. They were even fun to be around. I had never met people like these people. They were walking examples of Jesus, and they knew him personally. During this time, I was given a copy of Josh's book, *More Than a Carpenter*. As I dived into the book, I was blown away by the evidence for God's existence, the life, death, and resurrection of Jesus, and how we can know he is God. The evidence convinced me not only that God exists but also that the teachings of the Bible are true. As I continued to encounter Jesus, grow in my personal relationship with him, and experience his love through other people, I began to experience healing. My doubts began to disappear, and my emotions began to agree with the intellectual truth I had discovered.

In a world of suffering, tragedy, pain, unmet longings, and unwanted behaviors, we don't always understand why we have the experiences we do. But our experiences don't change what is and isn't true. If we let life's circumstances interpret what we perceive as true—instead of letting the truth interpret our experiences— we'll never experience the relational, emotional, and spiritual wholeness God longs for us to enjoy.

I know what it's like to face tragedy, suffering, unmet longings, and unwanted behaviors. But the time I spent running from God because of my unanswered questions and anger toward him brought no progress, no resolution, and no health or wholeness. It only furthered my unmet longings and deepened my unwanted behaviors and lack of satisfaction in life. But when I came to the place of not always knowing "why" but knowing "who," I found the hope, healing, freedom, and satisfaction that I so desperately craved. And it is so worth it.

When Jesus walked this earth, healing people, teaching, and inviting people into a life of wholeness, he had many skeptics and critics. One day, as he walked with his disciples, the men he had been investing his life in, he asked them what the crowds were saying about him: "Who do people say I am?" They replied, "Some say John the Baptist; others say Elijah; and still others, one of the prophets." (Mark 8:27–28). Then Jesus got to the point:

"But what about *you*?" he asked. "Who do *you* say I am?"

Simon Peter answered, "You are the Messiah, the Son of the living God." (Matthew 16:15–16, italics added)

What about you? Who do *you* say Jesus is? Each of us has an individual decision to make, a conversation to have with Jesus. It's one of surrender or rebellion, friendship or alienation. When we die, we will stand before God, and those who have given their lives to Jesus and know him personally will spend eternity in heaven, a place of wholeness with no more tears, pain, or suffering. Those who don't surrender to Jesus will suffer the consequences of their choice—an eternity apart from God and everything he is, everything good, pleasing, satisfying, and beautiful. But Jesus's invitation, here and now, is for you. Who do you say he is? At the end of Chapter 7, we described how to begin a personal relationship with God and gave a simple prayer to consider praying. If you've yet to give your life to Jesus Christ, we encourage you to do so now, before reading further. Will you weigh the evidence, consider Jesus's love and purpose for you, and make a decision today?

## Questions for Reflection

1. Before you read this chapter, did you think truth was significant? If so, why? After reading this chapter, what have you learned about truth?
2. In what ways has our culture's shift toward subjective and emotional truth affected your view of truth?
3. What bearings do the truths explored in this chapter have on your identity, value, and purpose in life?
4. If you wish to learn more, will you consider obtaining and reading Josh's books, in particular *Evidence That Demands a Verdict* and *More Than a Carpenter*?

# CHAPTER ELEVEN

# YOUR MOVE

Everyone is on a journey, and our daily decisions determine our destination. Most of us would probably say that we want to be successful. We want to change the world and make an impact. We don't want to waste our lives. We want to live whole lives. How is that possible without knowing where our daily decisions are leading us? So, where do you find yourself in this season of your life? Today, in this moment? Are you growing into the person you want to be? Are you maturing into the person God made you to be?

Early in this book I (Josh) shared how I was exhausted and hurting others because of unmet longings and unwanted behaviors. I was frustrated with the people I worked with, served, and called my friends. I don't know if any of them would have known it, but I sure did. When someone would ask me for a favor of some kind, I would say *yes* with my mouth but *no* in my heart. Over time I realized that many of the same people would return, asking for something more—and little wonder, because I was a "yes man." "Yes, I will help you pay off a credit card." "Yes, I will speak at your last-minute event." "Yes, I can help you with that." I would almost always say "yes," especially when someone seemed to be in a real bind. This left me frustrated, resentful, and bitter with the people I loved and wanted to serve most.

Eventually I reached a place I call the "Pain Spot." It's a fork in the road, a place where we face the choice between the pain of changing and the pain of staying the same. In the "Pain Spot" we realize that pain is inescapable, but that only one road leads to improvement. I decided the pain from my unwanted behaviors had become unmanageable. I needed to get help; otherwise I'd soon crash and burn.

I'm so thankful I found a friend to help me uncover why I felt so exhausted and how I could take some practical steps to get healthy. I didn't know all that was at play from my past and at work shaping my present, but I would soon figure it out with the help of a guide, friend, and psychologist named Dr. Henry Cloud.

My present behaviors were products of my past. Almost everyone who experiences significant unmet longings in their family growing up will perform to be accepted. I believed if I rescued someone, I was a loving person. That was not true. I was longing to be accepted because one of the greatest longings I had as a boy was to be accepted unconditionally by my father. That never happened, and as I grew up the longing only intensified. I soon discovered that I could feel something like acceptance when I would rescue my mom or sister from my father's harmful behaviors; that seemed to be the only place I could find what I craved. Over many years and repeated opportunities, being a rescuer became as much a part of me as my last name. It got to the point where *yes* was not only my first answer when someone was in need; it felt like the only answer. This was a recipe for frustration, exhaustion, and bitterness. Henry helped me see that my unmet longing for acceptance as a boy was driving my unwanted behavior as a rescuer as an adult.

Henry helped me understand the words of Jesus: "But let your 'Yes' be 'Yes,' and your 'No,' 'No'" (Matthew 5:37 NKJV). He helped me see how my frustration in the present resulted from me still trying to get my unmet longings from the past met in unhealthy ways. This not only made sense to me; it also gave me great hope when Henry said that every invitation to help or rescue someone was an opportunity to strengthen my honesty, integrity, and my relationship to the Lord. I knew it would take time and help from God and others, but after years of being a people pleaser and rescuer, I began to believe in a healthier, brighter, God-glorifying future for me and those I cared most about.

I wanted to stop rescuing people for a few reasons. First, I wanted to honor God by being honest. I wanted to be a person of integrity and say *yes* when I meant *yes* and *no* when I meant *no*. It might sound ridiculously simple, but it hasn't been easy. I wanted honesty and love to flow from my heart *and* my mouth. I needed to know that I could say no and still be a loving person, and that sometimes the most loving thing I could do is say no.

Secondly, I wanted to treat others with love and respect. You see, by rescuing people, I took away opportunities for them to grow. That was not honoring to God or to them. If a friend asked me to pay off his credit card debt, I would do it—and then watch him continue living above his means. In rescuing, I often fed the problem by "solving" someone's problem so this person wouldn't have to. Obviously, this cycle repeatedly hurt both me and the person I thought I was helping.

So, for many weeks, every time I faced an opportunity to rescue, I would pray and ask God for wisdom to know what to say and do. Often, I felt like God was saying not to rescue the other person from the natural consequences that arose from his or her actions. It wasn't hard to pray to God, but it was consistently hard to step away from the rescuing rut that was so well-known and well-worn by me. Hard as it was, I kept it up, praying to God, listening to his promptings, being honest with myself, and then letting my inner voice be my outer voice—letting my *yes* be *yes* and my *no* be *no*.

A third reason gradually surfaced. At first I primarily wanted to get rid of my unwanted behaviors, but then my motivation began to shift. I didn't just want to stop rescuing others or overworking; I desperately wanted to help others experience healing and live out their true identity. Helping others became the greater motivation that helped me take some of the hard steps to move from a frustrated rescuer to a peaceful friend. I wanted to really love people rather than use them and their gratitude to assure me I was loved and accepted. I came to experience the true love Paul wrote of in 1 Corinthians 13, when he said that love "does not insist on its own way" (1 Corinthians 13:5 ESV), because it considers the other person's needs rather than one's own needs. When I was rescuing people, I was primarily considering how I would feel if I said "no." I wanted to feel like a good, loving person. I was focused on my own needs rather than the other person's needs. Even when I thought I was helping them, it was all about me.

It has taken years, and even today it would be easy to go back to saying "yes" out of my need for acceptance, but here is the big difference: as Henry Cloud promised, I've had many opportunities to strengthen my honesty, integrity, and my relationship to God by turning to him and moving more toward health. In the process I've experienced God's unconditional love and acceptance not because of what I do—whom I rescue or help—but because of who he is and who I am as his dearly loved son (see 1 John 3:1). I knew, of course, that I was accepted by God and loved unconditionally, but in choosing the pain of change over the pain of staying the same, I was able to experience a new level of acceptance from God and others that met my deepest longings and is still changing my unwanted behaviors.

## The Consequences of Chaos

Can you remember the last time you decided to move away from something unhealthy and toward something healthy? Maybe it was in January when you took a good look at some of your unhealthy habits and decided you were going to try to move toward health in an attempted New Year's resolution. What was the unhealthy or unwanted behavior you wanted to stop? Now that you have it in mind, I want you to consider a deeper question. Do you remember what motivated you to want to move away from the unhealthy behavior and toward health? *The Oxford Living Dictionary* defines motivation as "a reason or reasons one has for acting or behaving in a particular way."[1] Using that definition, do you remember what reason or reasons you had for wanting to move away from behaving in a particular way? I believe that all motivation to change, at the most basic level, comes down to either pain or pleasure. The pain of an unhealthy behavior becomes too much to endure, so desiring less pain or no pain can become a motivation for change. Conversely, we may want to experience greater pleasure or satisfaction in life, so we take action to experience change for the expected reward.

Our unwanted behaviors have consequences that cause pain in our lives and in the lives of those around us, and the pain only intensifies over time. God will use our pain to wake us up to the reality of where we are and of where we are headed. In his book, *The Problem of Pain*, C. S. Lewis wrote, "Pain insists upon being attended to. God whispers to us in our pleasures, speaks in our conscience, but shouts in our pains: it is his megaphone to rouse a deaf world."[2]

Many have spent much money, time, and toil trying to outrun the universal truth Paul cited in Galatians 6:7 (NRSV): "Do not be deceived; God is not mocked, for you reap whatever you sow." You will eventually have to face the consequences of your actions. It isn't popular to say so, but it's not unkind. In fact, the opposite is true; it's unkind to pretend that there aren't consequences to unwanted behaviors and sinful actions. God has given you as a human, made in his image, a unique and sacred privilege: freedom of choice. However, that freedom of choice does not come with the ability to choose the consequences of your choices. There is an unbreakable relationship between the choice and the consequence.

God revealed the way this works in the accounts of the very first human family. When the two brothers, Cain and Abel, offered sacrifices to God, the Bible says, "The LORD looked with favor on Abel and his offering, but on Cain and his offering he did not look with favor. So Cain was very angry" (Genesis 4:4–5). God said to Cain, "Why are you angry? Why is your face downcast? If you do what is right, will you not be accepted? But if you do not do what is right, sin is crouching at your door; it desires to have you, but you must rule over it" (Genesis 4:6–7). Cain could have chosen to rule his sin, but he didn't, so his sin ruled him. He had the freedom to choose right or wrong, life or death, and he chose tragically, murdering his brother Abel and bringing judgment and exile on himself. How differently those brothers' stories would've ended if Cain had accepted the opportunity God held out to him, to deal with the pain of his unmet need for acceptance and approval by receiving correction from God and mastering the unwanted behavior that crouched at his door.

All of our choices, behaviors, and actions have consequences. Sometimes the consequences are subtle and small, while at other times they are obvious and big. Cain became "a restless wanderer on the earth" (Genesis 4:12). He suffered the loss of family and community—even his identity, a punishment that he said was "more than I can bear" (Genesis 4:13). That is often the case. The consequences of our unwanted behaviors can become more than we can bear. But they can be redeemed by God when we face the pain of staying the same and willingly, prayerfully embrace the possibility of change.

## The Stakes Are High

Over three hundred years ago, Isaac Newton observed what came to be called Newton's Laws of Motion. Seen as revolutionary in their time, we accept them today as self-evident descriptions of the way the world works, definitions that have led to countless other discoveries and technologies that enabled humans to fly—even to travel to the moon and back. His third law states that for every action there is an equal and opposite *reaction* (a universal law, by the way, that is true for all people, for all cultures, for all time). Just as there is cause-and-effect at work in the natural world, so the Bible teaches that our actions produce consequences, and both our souls and our satisfaction and success in life are at stake. The stakes could not be higher.

The consequences of not engaging your unmet longings and getting help for your unwanted behaviors will almost never decrease. Consequences tend to grow bigger and become more costly over time. In Cain's case, the first consequence of his sacrifice and how he offered it was rejection, but his reaction produced consequences, which grew more serious and costly as his story unfolded. It didn't have to be that way for Cain, and it doesn't have to be that way for us.

What will be the costs of not learning to address your unmet longings in healthy ways? Will it be worth it to remain stuck in your unwanted behaviors that take you farther, keep you longer, and cost you more than you ever imagined? That's what unwanted behaviors always do. They take you farther than you want to go. They keep you longer than you want to stay. They cost you more than you want to pay.

There are three primary ways we experience pain and consequences if we don't address our unmet longings and unwanted behaviors. The first consequence is shame, which we've discussed in previous chapters. Brené Brown says, "I define shame as the intensely painful feeling or experience of believing that we are flawed and therefore unworthy of love and belonging—something we've experienced, done, or failed to do makes us unworthy of connection."[3]

Shame only intensifies with time, since it produces more lies,

FREE TO THRIVE

unmet longings, and loneliness. Shame begets more shame. After I (Ben) gained more than 100 pounds from overeating in college, I began to try to lose weight. I'd look in the mirror and be disgusted with what I saw, feel immense shame, muster up willpower, and ask my friends to hold me accountable. For a few days, I was fine. But the cravings and desires to binge became unmanageable. I had been caught in a cycle of escaping challenges in life through the high that junk food brought me for years; the response to cope had been deeply wired in my brain.

A few years ago, having just experienced a long week at work full of challenges, I felt inadequate and irritated. I had prepared a sermon but was unhappy with it. I was over-committed and exhausted. I began to think of sneaking out of the house to binge on fast food. My roommates had just gone to bed. I felt excitement and pleasure from the mere *thought* of sneaking out. Before long, I got in my car, drove away, and indulged in some high-calorie fast food. The pleasure and high was temporary, however, and I quickly came down, feeling even more shame. I had once again succumbed to the cycle I had been stuck in for years. I went to bed that night sad, full of shame, feeling alone, and even worse than before.

The second consequence of not dealing with the unmet longings that drive unwanted behaviors is that you break the heart of God and hurt yourself and others. When we sin, we turn our backs on God. Like Adam and Eve in Genesis 3, we choose to ignore or dismiss him. Our sin inevitably leads to a distance in intimacy or connection with God. He doesn't get mad at us or turn his back on us, but by sinning we are stiff-arming him. Such choices break his heart, for we are his children, and like any father he desires a close and deep connection with us.

But hurt people also hurt people. When we experience pain, we tend to inflict pain on others: unreasonable expectations, short tempers, critical attitudes, unkind words, and so on. We don't make our unhealthy decisions in a vacuum. Our choices affect others. If we don't deal with our unhealthy patterns, others will have to. Our wounds become our weapons when they are left unaddressed. When you are unaware of your wounds, or unwilling to acknowledge and address them, your pain tends to overflow onto others. Instead of inviting them closer to be part of the healing process, you will more likely drive others farther away; it's a natural response to move away from pain, not toward it. As a result, distance from God and others will be the by-product of your pain.

When I was struggling with overeating, porn, and anger, my struggles with hating myself intensified. I was easily irritated. I hurt others repeatedly. I judged others freely. I pushed people away. And I hated myself the whole time I was doing it. The pain eventually became bad enough and the prospect of reward great enough that I sought help and found healing and freedom.

The third primary consequence we experience from our unmet longings and unwanted behaviors is dissatisfaction. We miss out on a life of wholeness. We may experience temporary gratification or happiness from our unwanted behaviors, but we experience increasing dissatisfaction. We sense that something has to change. We grow tired of feeling controlled by unwanted behaviors rather than experiencing the freedom we were intended to enjoy. We miss out on happiness, satisfaction, and emotional and physical wellbeing. We know we're falling short of not only our purpose and potential, but also from the reward of impacting the world around us, which is much more satisfying than any fleeting pleasure our unwanted behaviors can offer.

All of these consequences prevent us from experiencing the thriving life God intended for us. He has so much more for you. So let's look at the second motivator of change in an individual's life, which we briefly mentioned earlier: the reward of dealing with our unmet longings and unwanted behaviors.

## A Greater Vision

The other motivation to change is pleasure or reward. Everyone wants to feel happy and experience satisfaction in life, not just temporarily but consistently. The framers of the U.S. Declaration of Independence listed "the pursuit of happiness" as a fundamental, universal human right. In their case, that pursuit motivated them and many of their contemporaries to face hardship, deprivation, and even death. The desire for a better life for oneself and one's loved ones can be the most powerful motivator for long term growth and progress.

The Bible even says that Jesus was motivated by the prospect of reward. He faced the immeasurable challenge of betrayal, rejection, ridicule, torture, and excruciating physical, emotional, and spiritual pain—why? "*For the joy set before him* he endured the cross, scorning its shame, and sat down at the right hand of the throne of God" (Hebrews 12:2, italics added). He saw that the joy on the other side of the pain—a finished task (see John 19:30), achieving victory over sin and death, "reconciling the world to himself" (2 Corinthians 5:19), and exercising all authority on heaven and earth (see Matthew 28:18)—would be worth it all.

So, what is the joy set before you? Being freed from shame? A better marriage or future family? Being empowered to change the world around you? Greater connection and fulfillment in your relationships with God and others? Not living your life reactively and merely surviving, but truly thriving and enjoying all God has in store for you? Finally experiencing a life of wholeness?

As I began my healing journey, I had to grasp a vision of what God might do through my life in order to keep moving forward, one day at a time. Some days I wanted to quit. Some days I didn't feel like going to counseling, reaching out to others, telling myself the truth, or going to recovery group meetings. But early in my healing journey, I began to think about where I was headed. I refused to bring my issues into the marriage and family I longed to have. I decided I needed help; I determined that there was no looking back. I envisioned God using me all around the world to help others find healing and freedom from their unwanted behaviors. That future joy got me through the hard work of healing. Today I'm getting to live out that future joy, and I can say firsthand that all of the struggle was worth it.

Ask yourself, "What is the joy that God might be setting before me?" The Apostle Paul, after having gone through much suffering, being shipwrecked, imprisoned, mocked, and beaten, said that he had learned to be content in every circumstance (Philippians 4:11). How? He knew that his strength came from God. He knew that God would provide for him. He knew that he would one day be with Jesus in heaven and that all his hard work and suffering to share Jesus's message with others would be worth it. He knew the reward and pleasure of continuing in ministry, seeing Jesus heal and save people, and that all of his troubles were temporary.

Jesus repeatedly told his followers that their future rewards would be worth the pain of change. He said, "Everyone who has left houses or brothers or sisters or father or mother or wife or children or fields for my sake will receive a hundred times as much and will inherit eternal life" (Matthew 19:29). He promised a "hundredfold" (KJV) return to his followers. That's not a 100 percent return on investment; that would be merely doubling the investment. A "hundredfold" is a 10,000 percent return! No investment on this earth can compete with that.

This idea of a greater reward, a greater vision, and ultimately a purpose or meaning to get through the pain is not only biblical, but also supported in psychological research. In one of the most significant studies ever done on the relation between finding meaning in life through tragic events and traumatic symptoms, the conclusions were astounding. The study, conducted among Americans who witnessed the terrorist attacks of September 11, 2001, concluded that those who found meaning in tragedy were likely to have lower post-traumatic stress symptoms. Those who found meaning also had a reduced fear of future terrorist attacks. Their feelings of vulnerability were reduced.

However, those who searched for meaning, but didn't find it, were more likely to report symptoms of post-traumatic stress over the next two years than those who never searched for meaning. The tragedy remained meaningless to them, which worsened their symptoms.[4]

As followers of Jesus, we are always given the meaning in our suffering. We know that our sufferings—including the pain of change—are not meaningless but are achieving eternal rewards and "an eternal glory" (2 Corinthians 4:17). Suffering produces perseverance, hope, and character in us (Romans 5:3–4); equips us to comfort others in their suffering (2 Corinthians 1:4); and makes us mature and complete (James 1:4).

Other studies have revealed a concept called post-traumatic growth, in which those who have gone through intense pain end up living more meaningful lives than before. Child psychologist Ann Masten points to several key factors, including developing a sense of meaning in life as a crucial component to thriving after traumatic events.[5] Another study, analyzing the lives of formerly incarcerated individuals, found that "The presence of meaning in life is synonymous with a person's well-being and with positive attributes of optimism, hope, happiness, and positive social interaction."[6]

Viktor Frankl's book, *Man's Search for Meaning*, chronicles his experience of finding strength to continue fighting for his life in a Nazi concentration camp during World War II. Overworked, underfed, and attempting to survive the bitter cold winter with friends dying all around him, he began to envision one day being free from the concentration camp, lecturing to crowds on the psychology of the camps. All of his challenges became experiences that would inform his future work. He found purpose in his pain, along with a greater reward to strive for. In contrast, those who lost hope around him began deteriorating, succumbing to illness and mental breakdowns, and surrendering to hopelessness and death. Frankl survived the concentration camps and was eventually liberated by American soldiers. He went on to write books, earn his Ph.D., and give lectures all over the world.

God designed human beings to be motivated to grow and heal by seeing beyond the pain of change and focusing on the reward. He designed us to be motivated by a greater vision, greater meaning, and greater purpose. He intends for us to live a life of thriving, in light of a greater reward, as we find meaning in our pain. God wants us to know the joy set before *us*. He wants to set us free from our unwanted behaviors. He wants to heal our pain. He wants to use us in the lives of others to help bring healing and freedom. He wants us to experience greater connection with himself and others. He wants us to know our true value and worth. He wants us to boldly share with others his message of healing, forgiveness, and joy that is found in a personal relationship with him, a relationship that is available to all.

Jesus promised that when we surrender to him what we're holding onto, we will find true life (Matthew 16:25). When we lay down these things—unwanted behaviors, unforgiveness, negative core beliefs about God, self, and others—and take strides to follow him in all areas, we will find purpose, thriving, and maximum satisfaction.

Consider what it would look like to live from a place of positive core beliefs and your longings being met in healthy ways by God, yourself, and others, rather than living in the chaos of lies and unwanted behaviors. Think through what rewards and positive benefits you might experience on the other side of your healing journey. The following chart will help you consider some of the ways this could take place.

| Longing | Results of My Longings Being Met |
|---|---|
| Acceptance | Secure in my value and how much I'm loved. Not compromising my standards, schedule, or capacity in an attempt to get people's acceptance or approval. Not reacting to lies and coping through unwanted behaviors. Being able to rest in my acceptance rather than being exhausted by striving to feel accepted. |
| Appreciation | Knowing that God approves of my effort and is proud of me no matter what. Being secure in knowing that what I do is meaningful and matters in this world, rather than being unsure and always wondering if my life means anything. |
| Affection | Respecting myself and others rather than seeking out affection through unhealthy people or inappropriate interactions. |
| Availability | Knowing that I am worth people's time and love, and that I'm not a burden. Believing God is always close, interested in the finite details of my life, and willing to engage with me. |
| Attention | Being confident in my thoughts, opinions, and choices. Knowing how to get to know others, take interest in their lives, and celebrate the differences. |
| Affirmation of Feelings | Knowing that my thoughts and feelings are legitimate and part of what it means to be human. Knowing that I am understood, seen, and not alone. |
| Assurance of Safety | Free from anxiety, obsessive thoughts, and knowing that God cares for my every need and will protect me. |

Does this sound liberating? Ultimately, living from a place of met longings helps us to be secure in our value, have greater connection with God and others, and live according to our purpose and potential. It frees us to give more to others and love others more, since we can only love our neighbors if we love ourselves. Think about how many hours each week you might spend coping through unwanted behaviors, feeling shame, or dwelling on your regrets and hurt. How much mental space and time might be freed up as you find healing from these things?

What would it look like for you to have your longings met and be free from your unwanted behaviors? How might you experience greater happiness, satisfaction, and enjoyment in life? How might your connection with God and others increase? How might you experience a greater capacity to love and give to others?

The daily decisions I (Josh) made in confronting my unmet longings and unwanted behaviors determined the stories I would tell. It's been an exciting ride. I've been married to Dottie and enjoyed more than fifty years of marriage (and counting) with a woman I love and cherish. I have a family that loves the Lord and delight to see all four of my kids raising our ten grandchildren in families that place Jesus at the center. I have a job I love and am still passionate about, even after serving sixty years. I get to serve in ministry with a team that has helped me minister to millions as I have traveled to over 135 countries. I've had the privilege of giving over 27,000 talks to over 45 million people and written over 150 books. All of this could have been compromised if I hadn't found help in addressing my unmet longings and unwanted behaviors. I'm so thankful I was set free to serve Jesus and others from a healthy place instead of being driven by my unmet longings. I'm so thankful to be living a life of wholeness.

Looking back over sixty years in ministry, I can now see how high the stakes were. Though I will never know what could have happened, I cannot envision much health or goodness coming from neglecting my unmet longings and continuing in my unhealthy patterns. It was only after engaging my unmet longings that healing began to take place. I couldn't have done it alone. I needed Dr. Henry Cloud, my wife Dottie, and the countless friends who walked alongside me. I can honestly say that I feel like the most blessed man in the world. I have my faith, health, family, and friends, and still get to do what I love. I have said this for years, and will continue to say, "I want to love God with all I have, bring as many people into the kingdom as possible, and have fun doing it."

## Your Next Move

Throughout this book, we've explored the Wholeness Apologetic model on page 35. Wholeness and healing happen as you continue to live into the concepts we have explored. See "God's Design for Healing" in the diagram for a summary of how we heal and move forward in wholeness.

We've also shared about the *Resolution Movement*, and how those part of it are overcoming unmet longings and unwanted behaviors. We want to invite you to be part of that as well. Join the movement with us. Give this book to your pastor, youth pastor, or a teen you know. Check out our website (www.resolution movement.org) and pages on social media for more posts, videos, and resources. Continue getting equipped to overcome unmet longings and unwanted behaviors.

In the back of this book, you'll find a section called "Tools for Growth." This will help you take further steps to apply the principles of this book into your life. We know that information without application is of little help in the growth process, so we encourage you to use these tools. Go through them and share the results with a safe and trusted person in your life.

Finally, we've compiled further recommended books and resources that deal with specific issues we have addressed in this book. Check out the list of recommended resources on the following pages to continue to grow in overcoming unwanted behaviors and experiencing the fulfillment of your unmet longings.

We encourage you to continue this journey, experiencing healing and freedom, living into wholeness. Make a practice of identifying and seeking the fulfillment of your unmet longings. Get help and support for your unwanted behaviors. Take this process one step at a time, one longing at a time, and one day at a time. Jesus has set before you a thriving life into which he is inviting you.

# APPENDICES

## TOOLS FOR GROWTH

# THE MET AND UNMET LONGINGS TABLE

Use this table to identify the extent to which your longings went unmet in your life growing up. Doing so will help you understand why you might struggle to this day with specific unmet longings and help you to begin to find healing. For each category, respond with one of the following: Hardly Met, Sometimes Met, Mostly Met.

After filling out the table, identify which three longings went unmet the most growing up:

1.

2.

3.

# THE MET AND UNMET LONGINGS TABLE

| Longings | Mom | Dad | Siblings | Friends |
|---|---|---|---|---|
| **1. Acceptance**<br>to be included, loved, and approved of as you are, no matter what. | | | | |
| **2. Appreciation**<br>to be thanked or encouraged for what you have done. | | | | |
| **3. Affection**<br>to be cared for with gentle touch or emotional engagement. | | | | |

| | | | |
|---|---|---|---|
| **4. Access** to have the consistent emotional and physical presence of key figures. | | | |
| **5. Attention** to be known and understood with someone entering your world. | | | |
| **6. Affirmation of Feelings** to have our feelings affirmed, validated, or confirmed by others. | | | |
| **7. Assurance of Safety** to feel safe, protected, and provided for emotionally, physically, and financially. | | | |

What negative core beliefs might you have about yourself from these unmet longings?

1.

2.

3.

What negative core beliefs might you have about God from these unmet longings?

1.

2.

3.

What negative core beliefs might you have about others from these unmet longings?

1.

2.

3.

See "Renewing the Mind" on the following pages for ways to overcome these negative core beliefs.

# APPENDIX B

# RENEWING THE MIND

Do not conform to the pattern of this world, but be transformed by the renewing of your mind. *(Romans 12:2)*

We demolish arguments and every pretension that sets itself up against the knowledge of God, and we take captive every thought to make it obedient to Christ. *(2 Corinthians 10:5)*

**U**se the following exercise as one way to begin rewiring your brain daily. When unmet longings and lies come up, meditate on these truths and experiences. We encourage you to utilize this practice to rewire negative core beliefs about God and others as well.

## Step One

Identify three core lies you believe about yourself, God, and others (e.g., *I'm worthless, I'm unlovable, I can never measure up, I can't trust people, if I let people close they will hurt me, God doesn't love me*).

Often, these are directly tied to some of the painful experiences in your life growing up.

1.

2.

3.

## Step Two

Identify a verse of Scripture to challenge each lie (e.g., *I'm not worthless because I'm loved*, as 1 John 3:1 (ESV) says—*"See what kind of love the Father has given to us, that we should be called children of God; and so we are"*).

1.

2.

3.

## Step Three

Identify a time in life when you experienced the truth of this Scripture and when God communicated this to you (e.g., *My first year in college, I recommitted my life to Christ at a worship gathering. During that experience I felt so loved and accepted by God and others and experienced what it meant to be a loved child of God, as 1 John 3:1 says*).

Visualizing this past experience engages the limbic system, the emotional brain, the same place our experiences of unmet longings are recorded. This helps the truth of Scripture sink into our heart and renew our mind.

1.

2.

3.

# PROACTIVE SUPPORT

We encourage you to identify one or two people you can begin talking with throughout each week about how you're truly doing. You may want to go through this book with them, but at minimum we encourage you to use the following questions to support one another in the growth process.

1. Which of the Seven Longings are going unmet in my life this week?
2. What am I feeling and believing as a result?
3. What unwanted behaviors might I desire to go to in order to cope with these unmet longings?
4. How can I seek their fulfillment through God and others?

# ADDITIONAL RESOURCES

In this section you'll find great additional resources for various issues related to unmet longings and unwanted behaviors. From counseling organizations to support for your spiritual life, these resources offer great next steps to this book, helping you experience further healing and growth (for more resources, check out resolutionmovement.org/resources).

## Compulsive Unwanted Behaviors

### RTribe (rtribe.org)

An organization offering online coaching, articles, and support for mental health and behavioral health issues. Its online platform offers daily support, empowering a movement of connection, freedom, and integrity by equipping and inspiring its users.

### Genesis Process (genesisprocess.org)

The Genesis Process provides a biblical and neurochemical understanding of what is broken and causes our self-destruction. Through videos, books, small group resources, and events, this organization offers a groundbreaking approach to understand and overcome unwanted behaviors.

### *How People Grow* (cloudtownsend.com)

Authors Dr. Henry Cloud and Dr. John Townsend unlock age-old keys to growth from Scripture to help people resolve issues of relationships, maturity, emotional problems, and overall spiritual growth. In this theological foundation to their best-selling book *Boundaries*, they discuss key concepts to help individuals understand and overcome unwanted behaviors.

### IITAP (iitap.com)

The International Institute for Trauma and Addiction Professionals (IITAP) is a global leader among practitioners who treat addictive and compulsive behaviors. IITAP provides a wealth of articles and resources, as well as a therapist locator to find the best support in your area.

## Sexual Issues

### Pure Desire Ministries (puredesire.org)

Your safe place to find hope and healing. A biblically and clinically sound organization offering counseling, small group resources, blogs, podcasts, and books to help individuals understand and overcome the effects of unwanted sexual behavior. Its groundbreaking book, *Pure Desire*, by Dr. Ted Roberts, is a must-read and a great starting point.

### Faithful & True (faithfulandtrue.com)

A Christian counseling ministry specializing in the treatment of unwanted sexual behavior, support for struggling spouses, and guidance for couples who have experienced relational betrayal. It offers counseling, weekend intensives, small group resources, blogs, podcasts, and books.

## The Freedom Fight (thefreedomfight.org)

A Christian-based and neuroscience-informed online recovery program for unwanted sexual behavior. This resource offers an anonymous and tech-based approach to experiencing freedom.

## *God Loves Sex* (theallendercenter.org)

This book by Drs. Dan Allender and Tremper Longman III offers a truly liberating, godly view of holy sensuality. Pairing psychological insight with sound biblical scholarship, it brings desire and sex out into the open, allowing Christians of any age and marital status to understand sex the way God meant it to be.

## *Unwanted* (jay-stringer.com)

In this book, therapist Jay Stringer explores the "why" behind self-destructive sexual choices. Through his groundbreaking research, Stringer found that unwanted sexual behavior can be both shaped by and predicted based on the parts of our story—past and present—that remain unaddressed. When we pay attention to our unwanted sexual desires and identify the unique reasons that trigger them, the path of healing is revealed.

# Abuse and Trauma

## Allender Center (theallendercenter.org)

One of the leading Christian organizations specializing in support for abuse and trauma. This theologically rich and psychologically deep organization offers trainings, specialized counseling, blogs, podcasts, and books to help individuals find healing from abuse and trauma.

## EMDR (emdr.com)

EMDR (Eye Movement Desensitization and Reprocessing) is psychotherapy that enables people to heal from the symptoms and emotional distress that are the result of disturbing life experiences. Repeated studies show that by using EMDR therapy, people can experience the benefits of psychotherapy that once took years to make a difference. It is widely assumed that severe emotional pain requires a long time to heal. EMDR therapy shows that the mind can in fact heal from psychological trauma just as much as the body recovers from physical trauma. Check out the website to locate an EMDR specialist in your area.

### *Healing the Wounded Heart* (theallendercenter.org)

This book by Dan B. Allender addresses issues of sexual abuse across social, religious, and gender lines. He provides a biblically based path for survivors to find healing and restoration through God's help, love, and mercy.

### *Please Tell: A Child's Story about Sexual Abuse* (amazon.com)

Written and illustrated by a young girl who was sexually molested by a family member, this book reaches out to other children in a way that no adult can. Jessie's words carry the message, "It's o.k. to tell; help can come when you tell." This book is an excellent tool for therapists, counselors, child protection workers, teachers, and parents dealing with children affected by sexual abuse.

## Mental Health

### RTribe (rtribe.org)

An organization offering online coaching, articles, and support for mental health and behavioral health issues. Its online platform offers daily support, empowering a movement of connection, freedom, and integrity by equipping and inspiring its users.

## AACC (aacc.net)

The American Association of Christian Counselors offers articles, courses, and a large network of coaches and therapists in your area.

## To Write Love on Her Arms (twloha.com)

A movement dedicated to presenting hope and finding help for people struggling with depression, addiction, self-injury, and suicide. TWLOHA exists to encourage, inform, inspire, and invest directly into treatment and recovery.

## Better Help (betterhelp.com)

An organization offering online professional counseling in an accessible, affordable, convenient, and private way. Through its online platform, anyone who struggles with life's challenges can get help anytime, anywhere.

# The Brain

### *The Brain That Changes Itself* (normandoidge.com)

In this revolutionary look at the brain, psychiatrist and psychoanalyst Norman Doidge, M.D., provides an introduction to both the brilliant scientists championing neuroplasticity and the people whose lives they've transformed. From stroke patients learning to speak again to the remarkable case of a woman born with half a brain that rewired itself to work as a whole, *The Brain That Changes Itself* will permanently alter the way we look at our brains, human nature, and human potential.

### *Switch on Your Brain* (drleaf.com)

This book by Dr. Caroline Leaf offers breakthrough neuroscientific research. What you are thinking every moment of every day becomes a physical reality in your brain and body, which affects your optimal mental and physical health. Based solidly on the latest neuroscientific research on the brain, as well as Dr. Caroline Leaf's clinical experience and research, you will learn how thoughts impact our spirit, soul, and body.

### Wired for Intimacy (ivpress.com)

In this book, neuroscientist and researcher William Struthers explains how pornography affects the male brain and what we can do about it. Because we are embodied beings, viewing pornography changes how the brain works, how we form memories, and how we make attachments. By better understanding the biological realities of our sexual development, we can cultivate healthier sexual perspectives and interpersonal relationships.

## Spiritual

### Cru (cru.org)

Cru, the largest missionary organization in the world, consists of various ministries for teens, college students, young professionals, and married couples in your area. Check out its online videos, articles, and ministries to take the next step in your spiritual journey.

### The Cure (trueface.org)

This book offers a unique and biblical understanding of the character of God. Many of us couldn't measure up to a standard we created, so we convinced ourselves it was God's. We read his words through our grid of shame and felt ourselves fall farther and farther behind. We took it out on each other: judging, comparing, faking, splintering. We all need to understand who God truly is, for it impacts the way we live, love, and see ourselves and other people.

### Church.org

Find a church in your area and get connected to invest in your spiritual growth and serve others.

### The Unshakeable Truth (josh.org)

This book uniquely presents apologetics relationally, focusing on how Christianity's doctrines affect relationships. The authors ground every concept in the overarching story of creation, incarnation, and re-creation. They cover core concepts of the Christian faith and how we can know it is true. Topics include: who God truly is, self-image and human value, evidence for the deity of Christ, evidence for the reliability of Scripture, and how we grow.

### See Yourself as God Sees You (josh.org)

This book uses stories and Scripture to establish and remind you of what God says about who you are, so that you can discover and live according to your true identity.

### 10 Ways to Say "I Love You": Embracing a Love That Lasts (josh.org)

A book to help married couples learn to express and fulfill the Seven Longings in ways that will deepen and broaden a lifelong love.

### How to Be a Hero to Your Kids (josh.org)

This book will position parents to meet their kids' longings in healthy and lasting ways.

# JOIN THE RESOLUTION MOVEMENT

Many people today face unprecedented levels of shame, anxiety, depression, porn use, and body image issues. New problems mean new opportunities for healing. Brain science and biblical truth will give you what you need to change struggles at the root.

Join the movement of young people overcoming hurts and struggles, and thriving in life.

## WE OFFER

| Interactive Speaking
| Small Group Curriculum
| Follow Up Materials
| Books
| Articles
| Videos
| Podcasts
| Social Media/Web Presence

FOR MORE INFO AND TO JOIN THE MOVEMENT, CHECK OUT RESOLUTIONMOVEMENT.ORG.

Josh McDowell
A CRU MINISTRY

# ACKNOWLEDGMENTS

This book is the result of Jesus and people, and how they changed our lives. We acknowledge, honor, and thank them.

Dr. Henry Cloud, Dr. Ted Roberts, Stephen Arterburn, and Dr. Mark Laaser, for being instrumental parts in our healing journeys.

My (Josh) wife, Dottie. You have changed my life more than anyone and are my greatest source of support, encouragement, and friendship.

My (Ben) Northway Church & Watermark crew in Dallas. Your endless prayers, encouragement, friendship, and support in both writing this book and my life have been unrivaled.

Bob Hostetler for his brilliant writing skills, insights, and coaching, which caused the words in this book to come alive to you, the reader.

# NOTES

## Introduction

1. See http://www.resolutionmovement.org.

## Chapter 1: Legitimate Longings

1. American Psychological Association, "Stress and Eating," 2013, https://www.apa.org/news/press/releases/stress/2013/eating.aspx.
2. Shahram Heshmat, "5 Patterns of Compulsive Buying," *Psychology Today*, June 12, 2018, https://www.psychologytoday.com/us/blog /science-choice/201806/5-patterns-compulsive-buying-disorder.
3. Christina Gregory, "Internet Addiction Disorder," Psycom, November 11, 2020, https://www.psycom.net/iadcriteria.html.
4. Lea Winerman, "By the Numbers: Our Stressed-Out Nation," *Monitor on Psychology* 48, no. 2 (December 2017): 80, https://www .apa.org/monitor/2017/12/numbers.aspx.
5. Karen Zraick, "Teenagers Say Depression and Anxiety Are Major Issues among Their Peers," *New York Times*, February 20, 2019, https://www.nytimes.com/2019/02/20/health/teenage-depression -statistics.html.
6. Laura Heck, "A Generation on Edge: A Look at Millennials and Mental Health," *Vox*, November 19, 2015, http://www.voxmagazine .com/news/features/a-generation-on-edge-a-look-at-millennials -and-mental/article_533c1384-fe5b-5321-84ae-8070ec158f17.html.
7. Robert L. Leahy, "How Big a Problem Is Anxiety?," *Psychology Today*, April 30, 2008, https://www.psychologytoday.com/us/blog /anxiety-files/200804/how-big-problem-is-anxiety.

8. Josh McDowell Ministry, *The Porn Phenomenon* (Ventura, CA: Barna, 2016), 41.

9. See http://www.resolutionmovement.org.

10. Mark and Debbie Laaser, *Seven Desires* (Grand Rapids, MI: Zondervan, 2013), 13.

11. Dan B. Allender, *To Be Told: God Invites You to Coauthor Your Future* (Colorado Springs, CO: WaterBrook, 2006), 47–48.

12. Touré Roberts, *Wholeness* (Grand Rapids, MI: Zondervan, 2018), 12 (emphasis in original).

## Chapter 2: Your Seven Longings

1. Sally Lloyd-Jones, *The Jesus Storybook Bible: Every Story Whispers His Name* (Grand Rapids, MI: Zonderkidz, 2007), 260, 262.

2. Francis J. Flynn, "Gratitude, the Gift that Keeps on Giving," *Insights*, March 1, 2012, https://www.gsb.stanford.edu/insights /frank-flynn-gratitude-gift-keeps-giving.

3. Talia Joubert, "US Experiment on Infants Withholding Attention," St. Paul's Collegiate School Hamilton, January 8, 2013, https:// stpauls.vxcommunity.com/Issue/us-experiment-on-infants-with holding-affection/13213.

4. Joubert, "US Experiment on Infants Withholding Attention."

5. Joubert, "US Experiment on Infants Withholding Attention."

6. Mark and Debbie Laaser, *Seven Desires* (Grand Rapids, MI: Zondervan, 2013), 28.

7. Liz Mineo, "Good Genes Are Nice, But Joy Is Better," *The Harvard Gazette*, April 11, 2017, https://news.harvard.edu/gazette/story /2017/04/over-nearly-80-years-harvard-study-has-been-showing -how-to-live-a-healthy-and-happy-life/.

8. Mineo, "Good Genes Are Nice, But Joy Is Better."

## Chapter 3: Your Unmet Longings

1. Sigmund Freud, *Civilization and Its Discontents* (Vienna, Austria: Internationaler Psychoanalytischer Verlag, 1930), 77.

2. Arielle Schwartz, *The Complex PTSD Workbook* (Berkeley, CA: Althea Press, 2016), 11.

3. Christine Caine, *Unashamed* (Grand Rapids, MI: Zondervan, 2016), 120.

# NOTES

4. Dan B. Allender, *To Be Told: God Invites You to Coauthor Your Future* (Colorado Springs, CO: WaterBrook, 2006), 5.

5. Henry Cloud and John Townsend, *How People Grow: What the Bible Reveals about Personal Growth* (Grand Rapids, MI: Zondervan, 2001), 82.

## Chapter 4: Identifying the Unwanted

1. W. A. Elwell, *Evangelical Dictionary of Theology: Second Edition* (Grand Rapids, MI: Baker Academic, 2001), 1103.

2. Klyne Snodgrass, *Ephesians*, NIV Application Commentary (Grand Rapids, MI: Zondervan, 1996), 231.

3. C. S. Lewis, *Mere Christianity* (New York: HarperCollins, 2001), 44.

4. Lewis, *Mere Christianity*, 44.

5. Mark and Debbie Laaser, *Seven Desires* (Grand Rapids, MI: Zondervan, 2013), 105.

6. Multivu, "New Cigna Study Reveals Loneliness at Epidemic Levels in America," May 1, 2018, http://www.multivu.com/players/English/8294451-cigna-us-loneliness-survey/.

7. Alexis C. Madrigal, "When Did TV Watching Peak?" *The Atlantic*, May 30, 2018, http://www.theatlantic.com/technology/archive/2018/05/when-did-tv-watching-peak/561464/.

8. Ingrid Solano, Nicholas R. Eaton, and K. Daniel O'Leary, "Pornography Consumption, Modality and Function in a Large Internet Sample." *Journal of Sex Research* 57, no. 1 (January 2020): 92–103, https://doi.org/10.1080/00224499.2018.1532488.

9. See Mark Levy, "A Problem Well-Stated Is Half-Solved." *Compelling* (blog), Levy Innovation, http://www.levyinnovation.com/a-problem-well-stated-is-half-solved/.

10. Mark and Debbie Laaser, *Seven Desires* (Grand Rapids, MI: Zondervan, 2013), 111–16.

11. Lewis, *Mere Christianity*, 136–137.

12. Snodgrass, *Ephesians*, 237.

## Chapter 5: Listen to Your Longings

1. Peter Scazzero, *Emotionally Healthy Spirituality: Unleash a Revolution in Your Life in Christ* (Grand Rapids, MI: Zondervan, 2017), 19.

2. See http://cityonahilldfw.com/about-us/.

3. Ted Roberts, *Seven Pillars of Freedom* (Gresham, OR: Pure Desire Ministries International 2015), 157.

4. Mark Laaser, *Healing the Wounds of Sexual Addiction* (Grand Rapids, MI: Zondervan, 2004) 24.

5. John Perkins, *Dream With Me: Race, Love, and the Struggle We Must Win* (Grand Rapids, MI: Baker, 2017), 23.

6. Dan Allender and Tremper Longman III, *The Cry of the Soul* (Dallas: Word, 1994), 24–25.

## Chapter 6: What Your Brain Needs You to Know

1. Norman Doidge, *The Brain That Changes Itself* (New York: Penguin Books, 2007), 304.

2. Michael Dye, *The Genesis Process* (Auburn, CA: Genesis Addiction Process & Programs, 2012), 10.

3. Ted Roberts, *Seven Pillars of Freedom* (Gresham, OR: Pure Desire Ministries International, 2015), 233.

4. Doidge, *The Brain That Changes Itself*, 53–54.

5. Doidge, *The Brain That Changes Itself*, 63.

6. Doidge, *The Brain That Changes Itself*, 108.

7. Ted Roberts, Ben Bennett, and Brett Butcher, *Living Free* (Gresham, OR: Pure Desire Ministries International, 2016), 189.

8. Doidge, *The Brain That Changes Itself*, xix.

9. Doidge, *The Brain That Changes Itself*, 288.

10. Doidge, *The Brain That Changes Itself*, 64.

11. Caroline Leaf, *Switch on Your Brain: The Key to Peak Happiness, Thinking, and Health* (Grand Rapids, MI: Baker Books, 2015), 20.

12. See http://www.resolutionmovement.org.

## Chapter 7: You've Got the Wrong God

1. John Lynch, Bruce McNicol, and Bill Thrall, *The Cure: What If God Isn't Who You Think He Is and Neither Are You* (Phoenix, AZ: Trueface, 2011), 34.

2. Josh McDowell, *The Father Connection: How You Can Make the Difference in Your Child's Self-Esteem and Sense of Purpose* (Nashville, TN: B&H Books, 2008), 18–19.

3. *The Heart of Man*, directed by Eric Esau (2017; Sypher Studios), 102 min..

4. Jon Dorbolo, "Augustine: On Evil," InterQuest, Oregon State University, 2002, https://oregonstate.edu/instruct/phl201/modules /Philosophers/Augustine/augustine_evil.html.

5. John Eldredge, *Fathered by God: Learning What Your Dad Could Never Teach You* (Nashville: Thomas Nelson, 2009), 27

6. Sally Lloyd-Jones, *The Jesus Storybook Bible* (Grand Rapids: ZonderKids, 2007), 36.

7. Billy Graham, "Why Easter Matters: 10 Quotes from Billy Graham," Billy Graham Evangelistic Association, April 11, 2019, https://billygraham.org/story/why-easter-matters-10-billy-graham -quotes/.

8. Josh McDowell, *The Father Connection: How You Can Make the Difference in Your Child's Self-Esteem and Sense of Purpose* (Nashville, TN: B&H Books, 2008), 19–21.

9. Psalm 51:5; Romans 6:23; Ephesians 2:1.

10. 1 Timothy 2:4; John 3:16.

11. 1 Peter 2:22.

12. 2 Corinthians 5:21; Romans 5:8.

13. 1 Corinthians 15:4.

14. Ephesians 1:7; 1 John 1:9; Romans 5:10; Acts 3:19.

15. John 14:6.

16. Ephesians 2:8–9.

17. Romans 10:9, 13.

## Chapter 8: Seeing Yourself as God Sees You

1. Brené Brown, "Listening to Shame," TED, March 16, 2012, YouTube video, 20:38, https://www.youtube.com/watch?v=ps N1DORYYV0.

2. John Lynch, Bruce McNicol, and Bill Thrall, *The Cure: What If God Isn't Who You Think He Is and Neither Are You* (Phoenix, AZ: Trueface, 2011), 17.

3. Josh McDowell, *See Yourself as God Sees You* (Wheaton, IL: Tyndale, 1999), 21.

4. Kathleen Kingsbury, "The Value of a Human Life: $129,000," *Time*, May 20, 2008, http://content.time.com/time/health/article /0,8599,1808049,00.html.

5. Lynch, McNicol, and Thrall, *The Cure*, 33.

## Chapter 9: You're Made for More

1. K. A. Mathews, *Genesis 1–11:26*, The New American Commentary (Nashville, TN: Broadman & Holman Publishers, 1996), 213.
2. Naomi V. Ekas, John D. Haltigan, and Daniel S. Messinger, "The Dynamic Still-Face Effect: Do Infants Decrease Bidding over Time When Parents Are Not Responsive?" *Developmental Psychology* 49, no. 6 (June 2013): 1027–35, https://doi.org/10.1037/a0029330.
3. Timothy Keller and Kathy Keller, *The Meaning of Marriage: Facing the Complexities of Commitment with the Wisdom of God* (New York: Penguin Books, 2011), 101.
4. Brené Brown, *Daring Greatly: How the Courage to Be Vulnerable Transforms the Way We Live, Love, Parent, and Lead* (New York: Avery, 2012), 34.
5. Brown, *Daring Greatly*, 34.
6. C. S. Lewis, *The Four Loves* (San Francisco: HarperOne, 2017), 155–56.
7. Johann Hari, "Everything You Think You Know about Addiction Is Wrong," TEDGlobalLondon video, June 2015, 14:34, https://www.ted.com/talks/johann_hari_everything_you_think_you_know_about_addiction_is_wrong#t-202527.
8. Hari, "Addiction."
9. Victoria Woollaston, "Why Talking about Yourself with Friends Can Be as Pleasurable as SEX," *Daily Mail*, July 18, 2013, https://www.dailymail.co.uk/sciencetech/article-2368451/Why-talking-friends-pleasurable-SEX.html.
10. See http://www.resolutionmovement.org.

## Chapter 10: What's True for Me Is True for You

1. Merriam-Webster's Collegiate Dictionary, 10th ed., s.v. "truth."
2. Michael Wolff, "Trump Unfit for Office," interview by Katy Tur, *Morning Joe*, MSNBC, January 8, 2018, https://www.msnbc.com/morning-joe/watch/-fire-and-fury-author-michael-wolff-trump-unfit-for-office-1131721795518.
3. Merriam-Webster's Collegiate Dictionary, 10th ed. (1994), s.v. "truth."
4. C. S. Lewis, "Christian Apologetics," in *God in the Dock* (Grand Rapids, MI: Eerdmans, 1970), 101.
5. C. S. Lewis, *The Weight of Glory* (Grand Rapids, MI: Zondervan, 2001), 140.

## Chapter 11: Your Move

1. Lexico, s.v. "Motivation," accessed November 25 , 2020, https://www.lexico.com/definition/motivation.

2. C. S. Lewis, *The Problem of Pain* (1940; repr., San Francisco: HarperSanFrancisco, 2001), 19.

3. Brené Brown, "Shame v. Guilt," brenebrown.com, January 14, 2013, https://brenebrown.com/articles/2013/01/14/shame-v-guilt/.

4. John A. Updegraff, Roxane Cohen Silver, and E. Alison Holman, "Searching for and Finding Meaning in Collective Trauma: Results from a National Longitudinal Study of the 9/11 Terrorist Attacks." *Journal of Personality and Social Psychology* 95, no. 3 (September 2008): 709–22, https://doi.org/10.1037/0022-3514.95.3.709.

5. Michael Bond, "The Secrets of Extraordinary Survivors," *BBC*, August 14, 2015, http://www.bbc.com/future/story/20150813-the-secrets-of-extraordinary-survivors.

6. Francesca Flood. "Reframing Trauma: The Transformative Power of Meaning in Life, Work, and Community." *Journal of Psychiatry and Psychiatric Disorders* 2 (2018): 145–66.